WITH GENEROUS H·E·A·R·T·S

How to Gather
Resources and Funds for Your Church,
Church School, Church Agency,
Chaplaincy, or Diocese

Glenn N. Holliman & Barbara L. Holliman

morehouse

HARRISBURG • LONDON

The Scripture quotations contained herein, unless otherwise indicated, are from the New Revised Standard Version Bible, copyright © 1989 by the Division of Christian Education of the National Councils of the Churches of Christ in the U.S.A. All rights reserved.

First published in 1997 as *With Generous Hearts: How to Raise Capital Funds for Your Church, Church School, Church Agency, or Regional Church Body* by Morehouse Publishing. Revised and expanded edition published in 2005 by

Morehouse Publishing, P.O. Box 1321, Harrisburg, PA 17105
Morehouse Publishing, The Tower Building, 11 York Road, London SE1 7NX
Morehouse Publishing is a Continuum imprint.

Library of Congress Cataloging-in-Publication Data

Holliman, Glenn N.
   With generous hearts : how to raise capital funds / Glenn N. Holliman and Barbara L. Holliman.— Rev. ed.
      p. cm.
   ISBN 0-8192-2166-X (pbk.)
   1. Church finance—United States. 2. Fund raising—United States. I. Holliman, Barbara L. II. Title.
BV772.5.H65 2005
254'.8—dc22   2004023137

Printed in the United States of America
04 05 06 07 08 09   10 9 8 7 6 5 4 3 2 1

CONTENTS

INTRODUCTION

ALMOST THREE DECADES AGO, while I was a history teacher and the vestry clerk at our small Tennessee Episcopal Church, we faced what now seems like a modest problem of slightly enlarging our parish hall and repairing a roof and a wall. The estimated cost of everything was less than $20,000; memory suggests that our annual church budget was close to $60,000, certainly not more. As this seemed a tremendous amount of money at the time, the vestry members faced the daunting task of meeting these pressing needs while staying within our modest budget. After vigorous soul-searching and prayer, we launched a capital drive.

We managed to do almost everything wrong in that campaign:

- A few of us made all of the decisions and failed to share information about the program adequately with the congregation. We placed an announcement or two in the church bulletin, but we never held a formal meeting to call the congregation together to discuss the needed changes or to give them any sense of ownership of the vision.

- We did not engage in a feasibility study to ensure that people were in favor of the project and willing to give.

- We did not ask the leadership to make suggestions as to what giving levels people should consider.

- We did not make one-on-one calls. When it came time to raise the money, we wrote letters to everybody—almost the worst thing we could have done. My gift of $500 was one of the largest donations. Letter writing, while appropriate for small gifts, is no substitute for personal visits or small group meetings to ask persons to consider major gifts.

- We failed to set deadlines.

- We never sought counsel or advice from experienced fund-raising firms or development officers.

We raised about half of what was needed, and the vestry borrowed the other half. Fortunately, the modest debt was quickly retired, but it was a lesson to me in how not to raise funds. I eventually left the classroom to become part of the alumni and development program of the school where I was employed. A few years later, the Right Reverend William E. Sanders asked me to become the Planned Giving Officer for the Episcopal Diocese of Tennessee. Along the way, with training, education, and experience, I acquired the skills necessary to raise financial resources in church, charity, and school environments.

In this book, Barbara and I want to share with you what we have learned in our twenty-plus years of campaign management. Since we wrote the first edition of this book, our adventures in Episcopal stewardship and development have continued and grown. In this edition we have revised several chapters and added sections on annual church giving, planned giving, and chaplaincy campaigns. Read, reflect, and seek to know what God calls you to accomplish, and then join us in the gathering of resources to further the mission of our church.

— Glenn N. Holliman

ONE

Increasing Philanthropic Competition: The Challenge for the Church

WE IN THE UNITED STATES are a generous people. At the beginning of the twenty-first century, citizens were giving away almost $250 billion a year to charities, churches, public hospitals, museums, schools and colleges, and myriad other not-for-profit organizations, and this in spite of economic uncertainty and the war on terrorism. Approximately 36 percent of this bounty goes to church and religious causes.

While this number is certainly impressive, it doesn't tell the whole story. In the early 1990s, 47 percent of all American charity went to churches. In blunt, secular terms, religious giving is losing market share in the United States, challenging us in the church as never before to gather resources for ministry.

We're used to doing that. As Americans and as Christians, we are heirs to a great tradition. Ever since our ancestors stepped off the boat, we have been trying to build that "city on a hill," that elusive utopia. Whenever a challenge emerges in our society, we organize and form a group to attack that problem. It is who we are as a nation, influenced deeply by Judeo-Christian values.

Efforts to fix all the problems, though, and particularly by giving money to solve them, creates "donor fatigue," too many agencies and good causes chasing after the same donors. In the United States, there are nearly one million "501c3" (the Internal Revenue Service designation for a not-for-profit agency) organizations, three times the number of not-for-profits just a generation ago. Approximately 40,000 new 501c3s are created in the United States each year, an incredible compliment to the generosity and idealism of the American people, but the trend indicates the staggering reality of increased philanthropic competition. Individual churches, independent schools, lobbying groups, political organizations and dozens of other agencies, clubs, and charities all add up to an estimated seven million organizations that troll daily for our dollars.

A century ago, the church was almost the only "charity" in town. The Salvation Army had yet to fully establish itself, and relatively few colleges, museums, and hospitals dotted the country. The Boy and Girl Scouts of America and Goodwill agencies didn't yet exist. All of this has changed, and the competition for charitable giving will only intensify. We cannot assume that church members will continue to support the church as fully in the future as in the past. Many thoughtful people believe that they are also doing

God's will by supporting counseling centers, homeless shelters, and schools in their communities.

Understanding the Basics of Fund Raising

To position your church, ministry, church school, or charity in this myriad of competing not-for-profits, it is important to know the basics of financial resource development. Fund-raising activities include four types: Annual Giving, Capital Campaign, Planned Giving, and the Special Event.

Annual Giving. For a church, this refers to donations placed in the collection plate each Sunday morning, which finance the ministry and other programs and services that church provides. Churches generally conduct an annual pledge drive and count on commitments made at that time, as well as on additional gifts given during the year. Independent schools, colleges, charities, and other not-for-profit organizations seek similar donations by mail, telephone, and special events in order to underwrite annual budgets. Few churches or nonprofits could exist without this committed and continuous giving.

The Capital Campaign. Churches and other charities occasionally need additional funds for maintenance, remodeling, restoration, or church expansion. Supporters are encouraged to make capital pledges, usually for three years or more, in addition to their annual commitments.

Planned Giving. Supporters give extraordinary gifts in a number of ways:

- bequests in wills, the most common type of planned gift
- life income gifts such as a pooled income fund, charitable remainder trust, or a charitable gift annuity, which allow donors to receive income from principle, and tax deductions (At the death of the final beneficiary, the remainder principle goes to the church or charity.)
- life insurance, either as a beneficiary or contingent beneficiary
- real estate, including the life estate, which allows the donor life time rights, including a tax deduction, to a home, farm, or vacation home; at death the property passes to the church or charity.

Planned giving is one of the fastest growing areas of resource development in North America.

Special Events. Churches, charities, and political organizations hold high-energy, labor-intensive fund-raising events such as auctions, bazaars, bike-athons, barbecues, festivals, and other activities to supplement the annual budget or underwrite a capital drive. Although these activities build cohesiveness and strengthen bonds of friendship and commitment to the organization, a special event can never be a substitute for a comprehensive annual-giving drive or capital campaign.

Six Fundamental Steps

Raising funds, of course, doesn't happen without some effort and attention to detail, as the story of my first capital campaign in the introduction illustrates. Imagine the annual giving program or capital campaign as a wheel or a circle with six points—the real "wheel of fortune."

With the wheel in mind, imagine that you are a member of St. Swithin's parish and you are considering ways of increasing your congregation's ministry resources.

The "Real" Wheel of Fortune

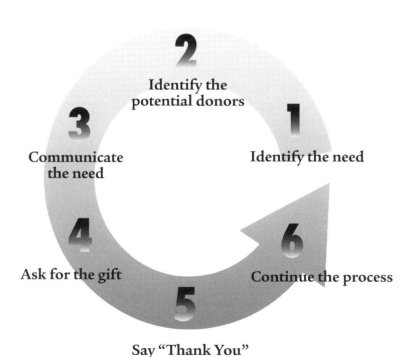

2 Identify the potential donors

3 Communicate the need

1 Identify the need

4 Ask for the gift

6 Continue the process

5 Say "Thank You"

1. **Identify the need** or opportunity, the urgent and compelling cause for which funds are required. What ministries and services are being or would be supported? For instance, perhaps you need to develop a nursery for child care, or you have a space that can be renovated for that purpose. Maybe you need more classrooms for church school, or seed money to begin a new family service.
2. **Identify the potential donors** within your constituency who can financially respond to the need, such as members of the congregation and those in the community who might support outreach services.
3. **Communicate the need.** Inform and involve those people who might have an interest in your ministry or program. You might, for instance, decide to run articles about the needs in the church newsletter, or invite the congregation to various events to hear about the potential programs. Do not assume that everyone understands or comprehends the ministries and programs involved. Seek advice about the proposed program from those who will be asked to contribute. People give when they have a sense of ownership.
4. **Ask for a gift** or donation to address the urgent and compelling cause.
5. **Say thank you** to those who have made donations or pledges. As a church, we are woefully remiss in expressions of appreciation for annual gifts.
6. **Continue the process** by identifying needs and opportunities, sharing basic information, inviting people to participate, and remembering to thank them for doing so.

Successful annual stewardship, annual giving, capital campaigns, and fund-raising programs follow this "wheel of fortune." Organizations such as major universities, hospitals, museums, libraries, and charities employ highly skilled, experienced professionals with sizable communication budgets to identify prospects and encourage gifts. Conversely, most churches, even larger ones, lack a development or stewardship officer to encourage gift giving to ministry, but that doesn't mean that churches can't be successful in raising funds.

A successful capital campaign or any fund-raising program depends upon communication, organization, and execution. You don't need a large, highly paid development department to make these a reality.

Ladder of Fund-Raising Effectiveness

At our office, we shudder when the phone rings and the caller says, "We're trying to raise several hundred thousand dollars. We wrote everybody a letter but raised only a few thousand. What did we do wrong?"

Though there are a variety of possibilities, in all likelihood the fundraisers neglected to prepare the congregation for the campaign. It is doubtful that they conducted a feasibility study, which is a formal survey to determine the congregation's readiness to participate financially in the proposed campaign. In addition, they apparently ignored the Ladder of Fund-Raising Effectiveness. This helpful tool reminds leaders to invest their campaign energies and time wisely. The top rung of the ladder is the most efficient way to raise funds; the bottom rung demonstrates the most inefficient.

One-on-One. There is no more effective fund-raising tool in the world than simply asking face-to-face: "Will you join me (or us) in giving?"

Small Group Gatherings. Leaders can also share their ideas at small group gatherings, perhaps hosted in a private home. This method offers a friendly

The Ladder of Fund Raising Effectiveness

1. One-on-one call by a committed person (or persons) on another.

2. Committed person speaks to a committed group.

3. Committed person telephones a committed person.

4. Letter from committed person to a committed person.

5. Committed person speaks to an uncommitted group.

6. Cold telephone call by a committed person to an uncommitted person.

7. Letter and publication by a committed person to an uncommitted person.

8. Print media.

9. Audio and visual media.

way to publicize visions of building projects or even annual church steward-ship efforts. It can be very effective in that it saves calling on people one-on-one. The downside of this activity is that solicitors are not able to meet and ask individuals privately to consider the appropriate level of individual giving.

Large Group Meetings. This less effective method brings a broad range of people with various generosity levels into a single setting—someone might pledge $1,000; others may be capable of $25,000 or more. It would be more productive to call on the potentially large donors individually and ask them to consider one of the leadership gifts. It is impossible to do this when they are sitting with a group, such as at a large, festive meal. Be aware that most groups have individuals who can respond at different levels of generosity based on where they are in their financial lives, and choose the solicitation technique accordingly.

Telephone Call from Committed to Committed. We do not recommend a tele-phone call from one committed person to another as a means of soliciting major gifts, but it is often done because it is convenient. This certainly hap-pens with smaller gifts. Someone might call and say, "I gave $1,000 last year to your cause. Can you give $1,000 this year to my cause?" A request for $10,000, $100,000, or more requires a private, personal meeting. Telephoning is effective, but not nearly as effective as a personal visit. It is important, though, as part of follow-up.

Letter from Committed to Committed. Further down on the ladder of effec-tiveness is a letter from a committed individual to another committed individual.

Letters are best followed up with telephone calls as they frequently sit unopened or forgotten on desks. E-mails can be deleted, accidentally or oth-erwise. Our experience indicates a multi-fold increase in gift support if tele-phone calls quickly follow the letters or e-mails. Letter writing is better suited for smaller gifts and is *not* a substitute for the personal calls required for major gifts.

Committed Person to Uncommitted Group. Less effective is an impassioned person asking an uncommitted group or assembly to consider giving. Leaders of charities and political groups often must communicate to uncommitted groups the importance of their cause.

Telephone by Committed Person to Uncommitted Person. Next would be a tele-phone call to an uncommitted person by a committed person. These calls are usually made at the dinner hour because people are more likely to be home.

Letter by Committed Person to Uncommitted Person. Most of us are used to receiving this type of solicitation. If you are a college graduate in this country, you receive about three hundred requests a year to give your money away. Most of these requests come by mail with some form of literature. You are probably receiving requests by e-mail as well.

Print Media. These are the ads in newspapers and magazines asking readers to clip out a coupon or call a toll-free number to make a gift. This particular technique generally isn't used by churches.

Audio and Visual Media. Last would be requests made through radio, television, or e-mail, asking donors to call a toll-free number and make a gift. More and more, national charities, as well as national denominational ministries, are using Internet websites to encourage gifts.

In this ladder of fund-raising effectiveness, the farther up the ladder you go, the higher the chances of receiving a sizable gift. So when conducting a capital campaign or even an annual stewardship drive, focus energies on personal calls and small group meetings. Just writing a letter may be adequate to finance the church budget, but not so for a capital campaign. Don't repeat the mistake that I made decades ago by just dropping an impersonal letter in the mail to prospective donors.

With some understanding of these basics, we are ready to explore more fully the three "donation" streams or legs that enable resources for ministry. Imagine a three-legged stool.

Resources for Ministry

Annual Giving   Capital Campaign   Planned Giving

Chapter Two will cover the first of these donation streams. Additional chapters will address the capital campaign and the planned giving programs.

Although the message in this book is generally directed at church resource development efforts, we have included specific chapters dealing with diocesan, church agency, college chaplain, and church school capital campaigns. We close the book with some thoughtful words on what to expect from your architect by a good friend and Episcopalian, Kenneth Graves of San Antonio, Texas, an architect himself.

TWO

Annual Giving for Churches: Your Annual Stewardship Campaign

THE GIFTS WE MAKE WEEKLY, MONTHLY, or as a total amount annually to our churches are the foundation of the mission and ministry of the church. Without the faithful giving of members, the work of our churches would grind quickly to a halt.

Annual giving continues to increase in the Episcopal Church, rising to over $1,700 per giving unit in 2003.

This "average" annual gift has moved steadily upward through the decades. According to published figures in the *Chronicle of Philanthropy*, it is the highest "average" annual gift of any mainline Protestant denomination. The Department of Stewardship and Development at the Episcopal Church Center in New York City, TENS (The Episcopal Network for Stewardship located in Wichita, Kansas), and many talented diocesan and parish stewardship officers have helped move the denomination forward in this area. Continuous training for lay and clergy leaders, provided by the above groups, and numerous printed resources have offered valuable guidance on how to encourage and upgrade annual giving.

Of course, much work still remains. For too many of our churches, annual stewardship drives consist of two sermons in November and an impersonal letter. We can do better than that. We normally recommend a three-part program for annual church stewardship drives, a process that can greatly improve your results:

1. Share a year-round theology of what it means to be a committed Christian steward.
2. Prepare and communicate a mission-driven budget.
3. Ask effectively.

Annual Giving/Stewardship

A Theology of Stewardship

Mission-Driven Budget

Effective Asking

A Theology of Stewardship

We all have a theology. We demonstrate this theology in how we spend our lives and what we give of ourselves and treasure to our families, friends, churches, and charities. As retired Bishop William Burrell of the Diocese of Rochester has often said, "Your checkbook can reveal a lot about your spiritual life."

Preaching the gospel each week could be considered an invitation to stewardship, but most of us need more guidance in sharing. Too often our checkbooks reveal our pursuit of material goods, and too little investment in sharing with others, charities, or the church. Giving to the church enables the sharing of the gospel and the ministries and programs for which our churches are responsible.

A number of year-round stewardship programs are available through the church press; examine them and select the process best for your church culture. Our personal understanding of giving begins in Scripture. Genesis 1:1 lays it out perfectly: "In the beginning God created . . ." Here we learn that we are creatures, not the creators, and all life is a gift from God. In celebration and thanksgiving we must share our lives and this creation with others.

Leviticus 27:30 introduces us to the suggested level of giving: "All tithes from the land, whether the seed from the ground or the fruit from the tree, are the LORD's; they are the LORD." The tithe remains woefully out of sight for most Americans. Generally, only 2.6 percent to 3 percent of the national income is given to not-for-profits.

First Chronicles 29:14 states emphatically, "For all things come from you, and of your own have we given you." This offertory prayer is a thanksgiving for the second capital campaign recognized in the Bible, the building of the Temple of Jerusalem during David's time. The New Testament also confronts us with sacrificial giving. Remember the story of the widow's mite? Or the rich young man whom Jesus urged to give all he had to the poor? One had little to give but gave much of what she had. The rich man had much but could not bring himself to give away even a little. As Americans, most of us are very wealthy, compared to the rest of the world.

The following is one of our favorite Scriptures, a disturbing story as it confronts all of us trying to save for and move through retirement. This cautionary tale warns us of hubris, of overbearing arrogance.

The Rich Fool—Luke 12:16–21

"The land of a rich man produced abundantly. And he thought to himself, 'What should I do, for I have no place to store my crops?' Then he said, 'I will do this: I will pull down my barns and build larger ones, and there I will store all my grain and my goods. And I will say to my soul, 'Soul, you have ample goods laid up for many years; relax, eat, drink, be merry.' But God said to him,

'You fool! This very night your life is being demanded of you. And the things you have prepared, whose will they be?' So it is with those who store up treasures for themselves but are not rich toward God."

Do you see yourself in this story? Substitute stocks and 401K/IRA plans for crops and barns , and this story barrels right into our faces. Like the rich man in the parable, we are confronted daily with the choices we must make in the sharing and distribution of our wealth, in the purchase of goods and services, in the quest for "the good life." As Christians, we are called by the Scriptures to self-examine and ask the hard question of how to acquire and share our wealth.

If we understand that we are the creatures of God's love and not creators of wealth, if we understand that all gifts come from God, then we understand that our salvation is not in this life, but rather in the love of God and our response to that love. For us, as Christians, part of our response to God's love is to support the ministry of the Christian Church.

Each of us is challenged to articulate and live out a theology of stewardship. As church leaders, we must also invite the congregation into greater understanding of the joy of giving. Is your church doing so on a systematic and continuous basis?

Prepare and Communicate a Mission-Driven Budget

In a typical Episcopal congregational profile, three categories emerge. We are indebted to the Reverend Hugh Magers, former Stewardship Director for the Episcopal Church, for some of the following insights:

- *Converted* (those who give to God)
  - This group gives 3 to 10 percent of their income and comprises 10 to 20 percent of an average congregation.
- *Committed* (those who give to the church)
  - This group gives 1 to 3 percent of their income and comprises 35 to 50 percent of the congregation
- *Uncommitted* (those who do not give)
  - This group does not give and could be 30 to 45 percent of the congregation. Nationally, 44 percent of all family units who are on Episcopal church membership rolls do not give regularly or at all, although they may put something in the collection offering at Christmas or Easter if they attend.

What a blessing it would be if all members of the church were in the Converted category! Perhaps if leaders established a stewardship theology coupled with preaching the gospel, the Committed (many will make the journey) and the Uncommitted will one day also be inspired to give to God. Until then, we can best reach the Committed by preparing and sharing a mission-driven budget. A mission-driven budget articulates, in narrative format, with graphics, photographs, and text (not just numbers), the many ministries of the church that are enabled by the gifts of parishioners.

We are all pressured to give our money to many worthy causes. If the church is to "compete" philanthropically with the other one million or so 501c3s in the United States, it must communicate more fully the *value* donors receive for their gifts. The Committed category, which composes the majority of a congregation's families, needs to know how gifts have been and will be used.

To better convey that information, you might break your budget into the following categories that define church. We use the acronym WOPPPEE (church should be fun!) to outline the programs and ministries of a church.

- "W" stands for worship, including the music program, that describes the central activity of any church. List all the worship services and music programs that enhance and inspire.

- "O" for outreach, and the many ways the congregation's giving spreads out to help others.

- "P" for pastoral care, the love and companionship we offer to each other.

- "P" for parish life, the ways we fellowship and grow together as a congregation, and the ways we offer the community the use of our facilities.

- "P" for parish administration, which insures the supervision of our people, programs, and properties.

- "E" for education of our children, youth, and adults.

- "E" for evangelism, our ministries of hospitality and church growth.

Take the time to explain fully these programs and invest appropriately in design and paper stock.

Compare the mail you have received from worthy causes and charities asking for your gifts. Some letters tell excellent stories in compelling fashions, and when they ask you to respond, you do. Now consider the explanatory materials most of our churches offer parishioners for understanding the annual budget. We can do a much better job telling our story and welcoming responses.

The Converted don't need these materials because they are, by and large, the leaders of the church, setting the budget and making the decisions, but the Committed are often outside of the decision-making loop and need the information. In fact, their giving is usually based on the perceived value they receive from the church. To some extent these are consumers. For example, young families desire adequate, clean nurseries and strong Christian education programs. Music lovers appreciate a good choir. Singles search for fellowship. People are seeking to know more about how the gospel can address their hurts, hopes, and families.

It is critical to communicate the value received through a mission-driven budget. For example, a church in Michigan has a large bulletin board that proclaims the ministries of the parish in three huge circles labeled *Stewardship, Education,* and *Evangelism.* Inside these circles are listed dozens of smaller ministries supported by members' gifts. This display or this inventory—a listing of ministries, programs, and services provided by the church—effectively communicates how gifts are used through the many ministries of that parish.

Often even church leaders are astounded by the breadth and depth of ministry emanating from their own parish. In a more cautionary tale of communication lapse, a parish vestry in Oregon was asked to list the ministries sponsored by the church. After recording over four hundred programs, the vestry members threw up their hands in celebration—as well as frustration! They had had no idea, even as leaders, to what extent giving to the church enabled programming and the changing of lives.

Whether it's an inventory or a narrative budget, provide your congregation with a written explanation of the ministries sponsored by and through the church. A large church in the Diocese of Virginia went a step further and invited the congregation to help build the budget through a visioning process. Leaders prepared and circulated a draft mission budget. They explained and presented in narrative fashion the challenges that the church faced concerning debt retirement, outreach, and Christian education programming. Through a brochure and questionnaire distributed at small groups and through the mail, individuals formed and expressed their opinions about which ministries to enhance or initiate. Those ministries that were most strongly embraced were integrated into the next budget. The congregation took "ownership" of the programming, and annual stewardship increased with a number of year-end designated gifts received as well.

How to Prepare a Mission-Driven Budget
Dare to vision:

■ Using our "WOPPPEE" outline, draft a list of ministries that could be enhanced or initiated by a 5, 10, or 25 percent increase in annual stewardship. For example, "If we averaged an increase of X percent, we could retain a full-time youth director."

■ Elaborate in writing how these increased ministries can serve the church and world.

- Communicate the current and proposed ministry inventory and vision to the congregation.

- Remind the congregation continuously throughout the year of the value of their contributions to the ministries.

There are several different methods of communication: Distribute to the congregation a narrative leaflet detailing your church's ministries. Use bulletin board displays, website postings, direct mail, e-mail, inserts in bulletins, newsletters, and, of course, oral presentations. It's best to tell your story over and over, not just during the annual stewardship appeal—although all of your work should climax then.

Ask Effectively

We generally don't ask effectively. Being busy, most stewardship chairs send a letter, often poorly prepared. In one prominent church in the East, the total stewardship drive amounted to mailing one photocopied letter with a photocopied signature. There wasn't a pledge card, only a tear-off response at the bottom of the photocopied letter. The carrier envelope had a computer-generated address label. No response envelope was included. No narrative budget or inventory was included. There was nothing compelling about the letter and nothing personal about the mailing. Is this your annual stewardship drive? We hope not, but too often that is the case for many churches.

So how does one ask effectively? The Ladder of Effectiveness suggests that dynamic, growing churches incorporate a blend of the following:

- one-on-one calls
- small group gatherings
- large group meetings (commitment meal)
- telephone canvass
- personalized mail canvass

One-on-One Calls

As appropriate, try to call on a certain percent of your congregation each year face-to-face. Sharing the vision in person and asking for a response remains the most effective way to gather major gifts.

- Prepare and communicate fully your mission-driven budget.

- Recruit one worker for every five recognized steward and newcomer families. In an "average" Episcopal Church, approximately 55 to 60 percent of the family units will be donors. Focus your energies on these folks, the *Converted* and the *Committed,* as defined earlier.

- Prepare pledge cards.
- Orient and train volunteer lay workers.
  - Label the pledge cards with the name, address, telephone number, and e-mail of each prospect.
  - Arrange the cards in alphabetical order.
  - Allow each worker to select cards for four or five families.
- Callers should visit with and invite their fellow members to join them in giving to advance the mission and ministry of the church. Schedule one or two Sundays for these visitations and publish the dates in church bulletins, announcements, newsletters, e-mails.
- Post a downloadable pledge card on the church website.
- Hold report meetings for callers until all calls are accomplished. These report meetings insure that calls are made in a timely fashion.
- Hold Commitment Sunday for the gathering of the cards. Celebrate with song, liturgy, and prayer for the receiving of these gifts.
- Follow up by mailing cards to those who have not yet committed. (You may need several mailings). Ask these persons to pledge.
- Telephone and e-mail prospects as appropriate.
- Send thank-you letters to all donors. This is something too few of our churches do!

Note: It is not always possible to mount this type of effort every single year. We suggest that you call on 5 to 10 percent of your stewards annually to thank them and liberally share with them the mission-driven budget for the coming year.

Small Group Gatherings

The small group gathering is another highly effective method to inform and harvest gifts. You should also continue to make leadership gift calls one-on-one, as appropriate.

- Invite members of the congregation to small group gatherings in homes, perhaps with a goal of involving a percentage of the congregation each year. These fellowship events are generally 1½ to 2 hours. The rector should be present with the stewardship chair. Serve light refreshments. Take thirty minutes of focused time to explain how the church is financed and how critical it is that members give to the program.
  - Share the mission-driven budget.

- Invite questions and encourage feedback.
- Distribute the mission-driven budget leaflet and pledge cards with response envelopes.

■ Send pledge card mailings with response envelopes to those who have not responded or who did not attend the gatherings. It is not necessary to invite every member of the entire congregation to a small group gathering every year. Try to reach at least a reasonable percentage each year, perhaps 25 percent, and keep your program manageable for your volunteers.

■ Follow-up by telephone for those who have not responded.

■ Send a thank-you letter for each pledge received.

■ Hold Commitment Sunday for the gathering of the pledge cards.

Large Group Meetings

Sometimes known as the Commitment Meal, a get-together of 25 to 40 percent of the parish can be an exciting festive meal and fellowship event in the life of the church.

■ Prepare and distribute the mission-driven budget leaflet throughout the congregation.

■ Prepare pledge cards for each family unit.

- Label the pledge cards with the name, address, telephone number, and e-mail address of the prospect.
- Arrange the pledge cards in alphabetical order.
- Allow each caller to select cards for four or five families.

■ Call on leadership (those known to give generously) prospects in advance, one-on-one. All leaders should commit their pledge prior to the event. Each year a certain percentage of the congregation should be seen one-on-one and thanked for their participation.

■ Recruit table heads for a large, all-congregational Commitment Meal.

- Table heads ensure attendance and distribution of a mission-driven budget leaflet, a commitment card, and a response envelope to each person. The table heads should invite people in advance to sit at their tables and, after distributing materials, should follow-up with telephone calls.

■ Hold the Commitment Meal and announce vision goals for next year, and progress toward those goals. Invite lay leaders of various ministries to tell their stories. All leaders should have committed their pledge prior to the event.

■ Invite a response at the end of the meal and/or encourage that all cards be returned by or on Commitment Sunday. If 50 percent of the congregation attends, that is a fantastic response.

■ Within a short time, hold Commitment Sunday and receive the commitment cards at an ingathering.

■ Mail pledge cards, mission-driven budget leaflets, and response envelopes to those who have not responded or were not able to attend the Commitment Meal.

■ Conduct telephone follow-up when needed.

■ Send a thank-you letter for each pledge received.

The Telephone Canvass

While it's true that we need to see some contributors face-to-face, the telephone remains a highly effective method to encourage pledging.

■ Mail pledge cards, mission-driven budget leaflets, and response envelopes two weeks prior to telephoning.

■ Announce that prospects *will not be telephoned* if their pledge cards are received by a particular date.

■ Gather callers in one place and have them telephone all those who have yet to commit and ask for a pledge. Calls can be made during mid-day; callers can leave a message if necessary.

■ To those not reached:
  • Follow-up with second mailing, as personalized as possible, with a hand-written note and hand-addressed envelope.

■ Hold Commitment Sunday to conclude the drive.

■ Send thank-you letters to all who pledge.

Personalized Mail Canvass

Finally, no matter which method or combination of methods you use, some parishioners will have to receive their commitment cards by mail. Some years, to conserve volunteer strength, your church may just mail the information. If you do, remember to:

■ Prepare and communicate the mission-driven budget leaflet.

■ Communicate details of next year's proposed ministries through newsletters, bulletins, announcements, parish meetings, and website.

- Mail to all members:
  - a cover letter that informs about ministries and invites a response
  - mission-driven budget leaflet
  - pledge card
  - response envelope
- Hand-address the notes. Ask the vestry to help.
- Consider creating a different letter for each of the following categories:
  - major donors who make a pledge
  - newcomers
  - regular donors
  - lapsed donors
  - dormant givers
- Place pledge cards in:
  - literature racks
  - pews
  - the narthex or welcoming space
- For unreported families, whose cards are still "out," mail materials a second, third, and even fourth time if necessary. Personalize these invitations to participate.
- Send thank-you letters to all who make a pledge.

Common Questions

- Can a parish do an annual campaign giving at the same time as a capital campaign?

  Yes, if the congregation is informed and educated, and the capital need is urgent and compelling. In our experience, if properly informed and involved effectively, church members will give generously for both annual stewardship and capital drives.

- Will a capital campaign depress annual giving?

  No; in fact, if done correctly, annual giving should increase as members become more educated about the needs and ministries of the church. We have worked with many churches that increased annual giving as well as achieved a capital goal.

THREE

The Discernment Phase of Your Church Capital Campaign

LET US EXAMINE NOW the next fundamental way of gathering resources for ministry, the capital campaign. We will explain the methods used to achieve the financial goals for your congregation, other local, regional, or national ministry, or church school.

A capital campaign can be broken into three distinctive phases. The first phase is discernment. The second is the feasibility study, and the third is the campaign itself. Imagine another three-legged stool, one like this:

The Capital Campaign

Discernment   Feasibility
               Study   Gifting
                                   Phase

Without balance on all three legs, the stool (the program) will not stand. So it is with a capital campaign. You likely will not raise capital gifts often, so be sure to do it right.

The Discernment Phase begins with the creation of the "vision statement," the reason that your church or ministry needs to raise funds. In theological terms, this is your statement of what you believe God is calling your ministry to accomplish. Discernment is the process whereby needs are identified, people are involved in the identification process, and the proposed plans are communicated to the church members. If done appropriately, discernment will create ownership and involvement within the congregation.

Discernment usually begins with informal discussions among the leaders of the church when needs have been recognized. Typical needs include restoration, renewal, or remodeling of facilities; construction of new facilities; program or outreach programs; and endowment funds to ensure the continued life of the congregation.

By far, the most common reason for conducting a capital campaign is to build a new facility or to restore or remodel an existing building.

Appoint a Committee

During the discernment phase, the church leadership authorizes the formation of a committee. This committee is sometimes called an exploratory, building, or capital needs committee. It is appointed to investigate the problems and opportunities affecting the facilities or ministries. The first thing this committee should do is to create a timeline and outline the tasks necessary to deliver a formal report of their findings to the leadership. With this timeline, they set deadlines for the activities and meetings.

Remember: ministry drives space. Consider the ministries and programs you wish to enhance or initiate. What type of space would be appropriate and where should this space be reconverted or constructed?

Inform the Congregation

The congregation should be made aware of the creation and purpose of the capital needs committee through newsletter articles, church bulletins, and announcements from the pulpit. It is never too early to begin a communication plan. In fact, you should appoint a communications chair at the very beginning of this process. Without information, people can not consider the emerging plans. You must explain to the congregation what you are going to tell them, then tell them, and then reiterate by telling them what you just told them. Even though you will do this constantly during the process, not everyone will get the message.

Often, outside help is needed to guide the leadership and the congregation in formulating and articulating what they wish to do. This is especially true when the plan incorporates more than the building program. For example, some other considerations:

■ Is outreach to be included, such as ministries to the disadvantaged?

■ Is money for endowment to be raised? If so, for what programs or ministries?

This often involves consultants experienced in ministry clarification, who lead church groups through a facilitation process. Newsprint, a magic marker, and an easel are part of putting on paper, and later into a computer, the collective thoughts of the church or other group.

Appoint Subcommittees

The capital need committee appoints the subcommittees necessary to study the problems and possibilities of construction and/or remodeling. To paraphrase the words in Exodus 35:10–12: "Come, all of you who are skilled craftsmen having special talents, and construct what God has commanded us: the Tabernacle tent, and its covering, clasps, frames, bars, pillars and bases. . . ."

Church subcommittees should be composed of skilled crafts people, of individuals who are knowledgeable about construction and/or any of the special purposes of the proposed effort. Opinion makers and philanthropic leaders in the congregation should also be asked to serve. They all need to adhere to the timeline that has been developed.

Involve Others

One of the tasks for subcommittees is to conduct a preliminary overview of the more obvious needs and opportunities within the church. For example, if the need is restoration, the subcommittee should make a list of observable structural problems, deferred maintenance, damage, and so forth. Then they can ask outside experts to make preliminary surveys and cost estimates.

If your church needs more education space, for instance, then involve the church school superintendent and teachers in the planning process. If a new kitchen is contemplated, those who use the kitchen should be appointed to the subcommittee. During a campaign in a church in a southern state a few years ago, a kitchen was designed without input by the men and women who were going to use the facility. There was considerable disappointment about how the kitchen functioned after construction was completed. Those who will use the anticipated space should have ongoing input in the planning process, along with the building experts.

Involve those who are potential major donors in the discernment process as well. Major gifts are necessary for the success of any campaign. In many church campaigns, 70 to 80 percent or more of the total goal will come from 30 percent or less of the congregation. In some cases, that ratio increases to as much as 90 percent of the goal donated by 10 percent of the congregation. Typically, donors to a capital drive represent 80 percent of the current pledging members; therefore, those members of the congregation capable of major gifts should be involved in planning or, at the very least, be kept well informed as the process moves forward.

The key word in any planning process is involvement. Planning, while guided by appropriate committee chairs and the clergy, must be embraced by the entire congregation and not just a few members. Projects fail if they are forced from above without the involvement of and eventual ownership by those who will be asked to approve and contribute to them.

In one church effort, a few people made most of the decisions about the program. When the feasibility study was conducted, the leadership discovered that the congregation knew almost nothing about the project. Another vestry had done all the planning themselves and failed to appoint subcommittees. The study revealed that 50 percent of those who responded had no idea that the church was even considering a capital campaign. This is an example of how *not* to prepare a congregation for a major effort, especially if you expect those members to make pledges over and above their stewardship gifts.

Remember the line from the movie *Cool Hand Luke?* "What we have here is a failure to communicate." If we fail to communicate, people will lack information about the program or will be unable to identify with it, and when it comes time to ask them to give, they will fail to make donations.

The Preliminary Report

Observing deadlines, subcommittees report back to the capital needs committee. The committee then prepares a preliminary report for the official leadership of the church. The leadership receives the report and may authorize the next steps, one of which may be spending money for architectural plans. The committee obtains draft architectural plans and cost estimates and passes them along to the official leadership.

Review the Plans

After the authorized leadership of the church has reviewed and revised the first estimated, projected costs, it is time to hold a congregational review of the plans. Some churches will ask the congregation at this time for a vote on whether or not to move ahead in the project; however, this is not the recommended procedure. Churches should wait and seek such consensus through a formal feasibility study.

The Need for a Feasibility Study

We often work with churches that desire to take or have already taken a congregational vote on launching a church capital campaign. We normally discourage a congregational vote, especially before a feasibility study, for two important reasons.

1. If the vote is taken during an all-church meeting, there is usually only a minority percentage of the congregation present. Some of the key philanthropic leaders and opinion makers may not be present. You may not even have a majority of the annual steward family units present,

and these are the ones that will most likely contribute. Historically, people who do not give annually to the church budget usually do not give to a capital drive. So a vote taken at such a meeting may not result in an accurate reflection of the congregation's wishes.

2. Congregations need the guidance of a feasibility study because many in the church are not capable of making major gifts to a capital drive. It is estimated that 10 to 20 percent of American families own two-thirds of the nation's private wealth. This minority provides the leadership and major gifts to most capital drives in this country, including that of your church.

This 10 to 20 percent of your congregation will normally give anywhere from 70 to 80 percent or more of the total amount most churches will raise in a capital drive, certainly those with ambitious goals. Many members of your church, including your leaders, either do not realize this imbalance or do not have this information at their disposal. An all-congregational vote, without the results of a feasibility study, will reflect the economic concerns and possible fears of the majority of your church members, but will not accurately interpret your financial potential for a capital campaign.

Invite, Do Not Command

We live in a country and an age that are known for individualism; it is very difficult to "command" people to participate and give. That's why we're so focused on involving the congregation. Goals are met when there is ownership of the process. In this discernment phase, participation in evaluating the proposed projects is vital. Through church-wide meetings, forums, cottage meetings, websites, adult Sunday school classes, women's groups, men's groups, bulletin boards, e-mail, newsletters, bulletins, and all other means, use every occasion to inform the congregation of the proposed plans. Be sure to keep those who have the capability to make major gifts especially informed. Broadcast to all, and narrowcast to opinion makers and philanthropic leaders. Do not allow a "failure to communicate." Set aside time for prayer, a time for meditation. This should be a time for quiet reflection and for continued dialogue.

Your next steps should include:

- Publishing the projected plans or programs in your newsletter, bulletin inserts, on bulletin boards, and by special letters.

- Displaying the plans (architect's model, drawings, etc.) in the narthex, parish hall, or other appropriate meeting place.

■ Providing detailed explanation about the proposed project by the architect and leadership at group meetings.

Incorporate informal feedback from the congregation into the plan's next revision, which will likely not be extensive if people have been involved as they should have been to this point. Major donor prospects must be informed of the plans as the process moves forward.

The process of appointing subcommittees, involving an architect, and communicating information to the congregation may take months, even years, of preparation and hard work. Mission statements may have to be fine-tuned, space studies and engineering surveys may have to be done, and many people must be involved in the process of deciding how to proceed. Only after this entire process has taken place will you be ready to engage in the feasibility study.

The discernment phase is critical and cannot be compromised. What follows are two handy checklists to help you monitor your discernment activities.

DISCERNMENT PROCESS CHECKLIST

Activity	*Date Completed*
Identify the Need	
The committee formed to identify the need will:	
■ Establish a plan of tasks and activities with assignments and deadlines.	_____
■ Sets dates for reporting findings.	_____
Involve Others	
■ Involve others in the planning.	_____
■ Form subcommittees.	_____
■ Communicate with professionals.	_____
■ Prepare report of findings to be shared with congregation, including:	_____
• identified needs	
• proposed solutions	
• cost estimates	

Communicate the Vision

- Hold (minimum of two) congregational   _____
  reviews

- Use other communication techniques,   _____
  including:

  _____

  _____

  _____

- Revise original proposed plans based on   _____
  input from the congregation.

- Prepare report to present to leadership.   _____

FEASIBILITY STUDY CHECKLIST

A client is ready for a Feasibility Study when the client has . . .

Activity	*Date Completed*
1. Prepared a draft narrative of the identified needs, justifiable proposed solutions, and cost estimates.	_____
2. Communicated proposed plans to the congregation.	_____
3. Explored financing for the project, such as borrowing from the bank, endowment, and so on.	_____
4. Obtained estimates of all associated costs, such as insurance, staff, maintenance costs, and furnishings.	_____
5. Researched and reviewed zoning and municipal codes.	_____
6. Informed the judicatory authority and followed appropriate procedures.	_____

FOUR

The Feasibility Study Phase of Your Church Capital Campaign

OFTEN OUR PHONE RINGS and someone asks, "Our church is planning a capital campaign. How much money can we expect to raise?" This is frequently the first question asked by clergy and lay committee chairs. In the past, a rough rule used to establish the campaign goal consisted of projecting an amount that was two to three times the annual pledge and plate offerings to the church. Although this practice can still be useful, beware of such folk wisdom in an age when church members are increasingly under pressure to give to secular capital efforts.

In reality, a church's donating potential cannot be determined without an accurate feasibility study, an intensive survey of the congregation. If the study does not reveal the potential for major gifts, the chance of raising an amount more than one, two, or three times the annual budget is considerably decreased, regardless of the perceived financial wealth of the congregation.

This brings to mind a joke: The minister said, "I have good news and bad news. The good news is that we have enough money for all our proposed plans. The bad news is that it's still in your pockets!"

The feasibility study should be done by an outside consultant to objectively ascertain the following information:

- Is the congregation supportive of the proposed plans?

- Which components of the proposed plans does the congregation consider the highest priority?

- Are members willing to financially support the proposed capital campaign?

- What potential leadership gifts are available?

- Is the proposed financial goal attainable?

- When should the campaign be held?

- What additional information should be shared with the congregation?

- Who should be the campaign chair and who should serve in leadership positions?

- Are planned gifts such as bequests in wills, life income gifts, and gifts of real estate, life insurance, and appreciated property possible and appropriate for this campaign?

A feasibility study ensures that no one can say, when asked to contribute, "No one asked my opinion." It also helps campaign leadership discover if they have set practical goals. Unrealistic financial objectives reduce gift support during a campaign as potential donors and leaders discover that there is little chance to fund hoped-for plans. Impossible targets make it difficult to recruit workers or for volunteers to make solicitation calls with any enthusiasm. Goals set too high lead to divided leadership and split congregations. People contribute to success, not failure, and a study is the best way to ensure that the congregation finds the plans acceptable and supports them.

And yet, some churches are reluctant to invest in a study. Some capital campaign firms, even to this day, will initiate campaigns and hope the goals can be obtained using standard fund-raising methods, along with much prayer and faith. Prayer and faith are important, paramount for a church congregation, but consider the wisdom of Jesus found in Luke:

"For which of you, intending to build a tower, does not first sit down and estimate the cost, to see whether he has enough to complete it? Otherwise, when he has laid a foundation and is not able to finish, all who see it will begin to ridicule him, saying, 'This fellow began to build and was not able to finish'"(14:28–30).

A feasibility study is the only way we know to ensure that a modern-day committee avoids the plight of not being able to finish its "tower." The church needs to ascertain the financial reality of its project, as well as the willingness and readiness of a congregation to give.

The Importance of a Feasibility Study

A struggling congregation in the southwestern part of the United States had an annual budget of $90,000. A small preschool was adjacent to the church. The official leadership voted six to five to authorize us to do a feasibility study to test for $650,000 for capital improvements for both the church and school, approximately seven times the annual pledge and plate of the church. Remember the rough rule is that a church can raise two to three times its annual giving. Obviously this was an ambitious goal, as the small preschool constituency could be expected to give little, but we hoped we could find at least some resources and adjust the plans accordingly.

During the study process we interviewed one man who said, "I'll give $50,000." Then we thought, "Maybe we could raise $200,000."

When we were selecting individuals to be interviewed in the study, people suggested that we talk to a community leader who had a grandchild in the preschool. She was not a member of the church, but during the interview she said she would give $50,000. In addition, she wanted to issue a challenge to the church and school: She would give a total of $350,000 if leadership could raise $300,000—more than a one-for-one match.

The church and school rose to the occasion. The full amount was raised, and the plans went forward. Guess what happened then? There were cost overruns. The church went back to the same woman, and she gave another $250,000. This generous woman gave 70% of the entire cost of the program.

If there had not been a study in this case, the church and school leadership would not have known that the resources were available to move ahead with their ambitious program.

Another study illustration comes to mind—a strong, middle-class, suburban church in the Midwest. Leadership planned to spend $400,000 to remodel the church, but the study revealed that the congregation was ambivalent about the proposed plans and would not give an amount even equal to the annual pledge and plate of the church, which in this case, was approximately $400,000. We took this information to the leadership, who were chagrined that the congregation was so unsupportive of what they were trying to do. At that point, several members of the vestry, silent heretofore, expressed their own concerns about the project. Thus the program did not go forward. Leadership went back to the drawing board using the feedback from the study. This time they involved more members from the congregation in the planning stages. Eventually they came up with plans that were much more acceptable to the congregation. The moral of the story is to discern thoroughly, communicate well, listen to your congregation, accept what they have to say and how much they are willing to give, and adjust accordingly.

Often, as a result of a study, plans do have to be revised. The financial resources may not be available to support the dreams of the leadership. By all means, have a vision. Just recognize that the vision may have to be divided into phases and done over a longer period of time than initially desired. Certainly it is all right to test for an amount equal to two to ten times your annual giving. If you have some potential major gifts, go ahead and share the plans and invite a response. Just be ready to break an ambitious program into parts or phases if the funds cannot be raised all at once. You are sharing a long-range vision.

It is important that a congregation feels successful. A study is the only way to ensure that you are dealing with philanthropic reality prior to the beginning of a campaign. God moves in mysterious ways, and often systematically.

What to Do with the Study Results

Church leadership should receive the study and make a decision to proceed with the campaign or not. Assuming the study is positive, your Capital Needs Committee should recommend the appropriate goal for the project, based on what they've learned in the study. If your vision has been too ambitious, take time to review what parts of the plan to pursue. Input concerning prioritization of the program should be gleaned from your study. If leadership gifts are not discovered in a study, the project will have to be altered or postponed. Allow time for this revised process to occur before launching the solicitation of gifts. Remember, raising the goal does not mean people will give more.

If you are considering a construction program, keep in mind that it takes time for an architect to revise plans, obtain new cost estimates, and then communicate these changes to the church membership. Often, this process takes months, and it will necessitate a delay to the proposed start of the campaign.

In some cases accomplishing the whole program may necessitate borrowing money. In the feasibility study, this should be broached to the congregation so that members have time to consider the information and to understand what impact debt service might have on the annual budget.

Some churches feel very reluctant to borrow; it is not a problem for others. Be aware of how much you can prudently borrow, and make sure that you are able to repay the debt on a timely schedule, whether it takes five years or thirty years. One Midwest church overbuilt in an effort to attract more people. Unfortunately, the congregation did not grow as planned and the local economy slipped into a recession. The church was forced to use two-thirds of its annual income not for debt retirement, but merely to pay the interest on the debt, which devastated both programming and ministry. Ultimately, the church required a debt reduction campaign—generally the most difficult campaign for which to raise funds. So be careful, choose wisely, and do not over-commit yourself in terms of a mortgage.

Feasibility Studies Can Differ

There are different kinds of feasibility studies. Firms differ on processes and how surveys are conducted. As you interview potential consultants, ask to see copies of studies they have done. Ask consultants to describe their basic questions and why these questions are asked. Also, ask the following:

How many members of the congregation are polled? A few? Everyone? Are people asked individually what their personal donation might be or is it a "group guess"? How accurate are the firm's studies? What percentage of studies lead to campaigns? Is the survey done with integrity? What parts of the study remain confidential? What can later be shared with the congregation or constituency? Is the confidential data available to church leaders if the firm is *not* hired to direct the campaign? Is the study designed for a non-church constituency or is it shaped for a church audience?

Finally, ask for references. Talk to other churches and ascertain how well the study process and results worked out. Once your discernment phase and feasibility study are complete, you're ready to begin the campaign, or the Gifting Phase, itself.

FIVE

The Gifting Phase for Your Church

LET US NOW MOVE from Discernment and the Feasibility Study phases and discuss how to solicit gifts and pledges. We divide this process into five parts:

- Preparation and Planning

- Leadership Recruitment

- Advance Gifts

- Congregational Gifts

- Celebration and Acknowledgment

As with any activity, one must assemble people and plans. Campaigns must begin and end. A thousand separate activities must occur in a relatively short time, but here is a "snapshot" of how a typical campaign unfolds. What follows is a typical timeline for a church campaign.

Preparation and Planning—Leadership Recruitment: Months One and Two

- Finalize case statement and goal.

- Establish and approve campaign budget.

- Determine campaign theme.

- Establish campaign office.

- Prepare and publish a volunteer handbook that includes the organizational chart, campaign calendar, Gifts Essential Chart, and job descriptions for volunteers.

- Develop communications plan.

- Research and compile lists of donors and campaign leadership prospects.

- Prepare materials, including brochure, pledge card, letterhead, and other necessary items.

- Identify, recruit, and orient campaign leadership.

■ Conduct Advance Gift Evaluation.

■ Identify and recruit leadership for divisional and support committees.

■ Begin communication and cultivation activities.

Advance Gifts: Months Two and Three

■ Direct Advance Gifts worker training.

■ Monitor Advance Gifts solicitation efforts.

■ Organize, schedule, and direct regular report sessions.

■ Implement acknowledgment systems and procedures.

■ Contact planned giving prospects, if appropriate.

Congregational Gifts: Months Three and Four

■ Orient Congregational Gifts leadership.

■ Launch Congregational Gifts solicitation with kick-off event and activities.

■ Direct Congregational Gifts worker training sessions.

■ Commission volunteers on Dedication Sunday.

■ Monitor Congregational Gifts solicitation efforts.

■ Complete Advance Gifts phase.

■ Finalize planned gifts, if appropriate.

■ Supervise acknowledgment of all gifts.

Celebration and Acknowledgment: Months Four and Five

■ Provide leadership with accurate and complete records and instructions for pledge collection.

■ Hold Celebration Sunday and a volunteer recognition event.

Getting Started: Preparation and Planning

As you begin your campaign activities, you must first organize a campaign office. It is a good idea to hire a part-time clerical person to assist with the tasks, as this work is usually over and above what the current church secretary can handle. Temp agencies are good sources for this kind of work, or you could also talk to another church's minister about someone in their congregation who would like some part-time work. It is unwise to hire parishioners—if the business relationship doesn't work, it will be difficult to dismiss them. Also, some church members are not comfortable with the idea of fellow members knowing about their financial situations. At any rate, the person you hire should be very organized and detail-oriented and should possess good people skills. This clerical person will be communicating with your volunteers, organizing events, preparing campaign memos, and logging and sending acknowledgments to donors. How much clerical time is needed depends on the size of your church: for some small congregations, only ten to fifteen hours a week are necessary; for larger churches, full-time help may be required.

Equip a room with a computer with e-mail capabilities, appropriate software for tracking the campaign, and a telephone with messaging capabilities. Have access to a photocopier and fax machine.

At the top of your organizational chart will be the *Clergy* and *Vestry* leadership. Next will be the *Campaign Chair* or, preferably, co-chairs. By sharing the responsibilities you can involve more people and use the leadership to cover the diversity of the church membership. Normally, the organization will branch off into two sections. One section will be the *Advance Gifts Division,* including a chair or co-chairs and committee members to make the Advance Gifts calls. This division will solicit the larger gifts, typically $5,000 and above, in addition to gifts from the rector and campaign leadership. On the other side of the chart will be the *Congregational Gifts Division,* including a congregational chair or co-chairs and the workers who solicit the gifts from the remainder of the membership. If the church is large, you might need a level of captains to recruit the solicitors.

On a few occasions, there should be a *Community Gifts Division* for those churches that may have the ability, due to outreach programs or interest in historic preservation in the community, to reach outside of the congregation for financial support.

Support committees also are necessary to strengthen the campaign. These groups include: A *Spiritual Emphasis* group to remind the congregation and the leadership that this is not merely fund raising but an effort to harvest the resources necessary to carry out the ministry of Jesus Christ. The *Kick-Off Event* Chair and Committee will organize the major event that brings the whole congregation together to celebrate the launch of the campaign.

In some cases, a *Planned Giving* Committee is created to inform the congregation about what planned gifts are and how to consider them. This program often continues on after the formal campaign is completed.

A *Communication* Committee is necessary to ensure that information about the program is shared with the congregation in as many different ways

A SAMPLE ORGANIZATION CHART FOR A TYPICAL CHURCH CAMPAIGN

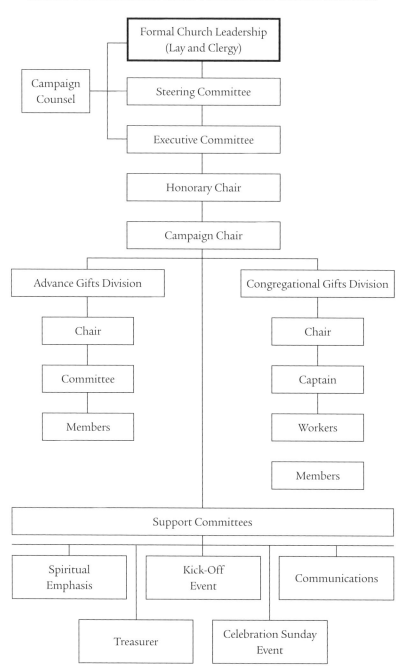

as possible. Use the church newsletter, Sunday bulletin, bulletin boards, website, e-mails, messages from the pulpit, and testimonies from parishioners during announcement time. Continue to speak to the Christian education classes. Hold meetings. Do whatever it takes to keep informing the congregation about the current campaign progress and activities.

The *Celebration Sunday* chair and committee ensure that the campaign volunteers are recognized and thanked, and that the solicitation has formally concluded and the gifts are celebrated.

Prepare Campaign Printed Materials

Volunteer Handbook. Once you determine the campaign objectives and amount of the goal, you can prepare a handbook for the volunteers you enlist. (This is also a useful tool for recruiting your leadership.)

The *Volunteer Handbook* has these components:

- campaign objective and goal

- Gifts Essential Chart

- organizational chart

- leadership job descriptions

- campaign calendar (timeline of activities)

Campaign Brochure. In addition to your volunteer handbook, which you can usually produce attractively on your own, you will need a brochure to simply describe the campaign goal and objectives. Although the discernment and feasibility study phases have communicated your needs throughout the congregation, it is imperative to inform everyone what final plans, programs, and costs have been determined as the campaign objectives. In just a few pages, articulate why your church needs to raise money to build or restore. Include photographs and, if appropriate to the size of the project, drawings or architectural renderings. It's best to include the Gifts Essential Chart, the campaign prayer, and names and roles of those in leadership positions. The extent of the brochure will vary according to the church size and culture.

Larger, more involved campaigns may require more elaborate brochures. You might select a design firm that is familiar with fund raising to produce campaign materials. A brochure is more than just a public relations piece; it must use development language to encourage greater gifting. These collateral materials may take anywhere from three to six weeks to prepare from beginning to end. Be sure everything is completed before your first Advance Gifts Worker Training Meeting so you can share the brochures with the volunteers.

Pledge Card. There must be a pledge card. If the Gifts Essential Chart is not included in the brochure, it should be shown on the pledge card. In this way prospective donors can see the sizes and numbers of gifts necessary to reach the campaign goal. These sample charts suggest the giving levels necessary in order to achieve your campaign goal. Usually the lead gift is 15 to 20 percent of the goal. The total number of gifts necessary should not exceed the number of pledging and giving units in your church. Traditionally, only 80 percent of those who give regularly to stewardship make gifts to a capital drive.

A Sample Gifts Essential Chart
A goal of $500,000 for a church with 300-400 families

Size of gift	# Needed	Cumulative Total
$75,000	1	$75,000
50,000	1	125,000
25,000	2	175,000
10,000	3	205,000
5,000	10	255,000
3,000	30	345,000
1,000	100	445,000
Below $1,000	Many	Goal Achieved

A goal of $500,000 for a church with 100-200 families

Size of gift	# Needed	Cumulative Total
$100,000	1	$100,000
75,000	1	175,000
50,000	1	225,000
25,000	1	250,000
10,000	5	300,000
5,000	10	350,000
3,000	25	425,000
1,000	50	475,000
Below $500	Many	Goal Achieved

The following items are normally included on a pledge card:

- campaign theme and logo
- area for name, address, telephone number, and e-mail address

- area for the amount of the pledge, amount paid (if a check was included at the time of making the commitment), and remaining outstanding balance

- indication of donation schedule, such as weekly, monthly, quarterly, or annually

- the Gifts Essential Chart, which reminds donors of what gifts are necessary to achieve success

- the campaign prayer, so people can prayerfully consider a gift

The paper stock and colors of the pledge card should complement the campaign brochure. Including your brochure on your church website is helpful as well.

Other printed materials, such as meeting agendas, gift acknowledgments, and quarterly reminder statements, are usually produced on campaign letterhead that includes the names of the leadership and their positions. This separates communication from regular church business and annual stewardship communications. Note cards can be produced with the campaign logo for thank-you notes, invitations to events, and other special uses.

Often, youth groups or creative members of a parish will make "goal thermometers" to show progress during the Congregational Gifts Phase. Such graphics should be located in prominent places so people will see them often.

In addition, youth can make banners and place mats, for example, during Sunday school sessions. This is a good way to get them involved and understand how a campaign relates to stewardship.

Leaders and Their Roles

The process of recruiting leaders can be a difficult and lengthy process. In order to make this task a bit easier, refer to the job descriptions in the organizational chart. Recruiting committee members is the first task leadership should undertake. We've discovered that appointing co-chairs for all the positions strengthens involvement and diversity.

The first committee member you should identify and recruit is the Campaign Chair, whose job it will be to motivate the volunteers and church members during the campaign. This person should have credibility and visibility within the church.

The Advance Gifts Division

After the top tier of leadership has been determined, you should next identify and recruit the Advance Gifts Chair. This person must be able to make a sizeable gift and have the ability to ask others to make large gifts.

It is necessary to consider Advance Gifts as a separate division. This group sets the momentum for the campaign and usually raises 70 to 80 percent or more of the goal before the campaign even goes before the congregation. When you launch the campaign at the Kick-Off Event, you will announce the amount already raised by the Advance Gifts Division so that the goal will appear more achievable to the remainder of the congregation.

Just as in any community or charity campaign, leaders must go to a certain percentage of the church population early and ask for their consideration of a major gift. Most people know when they are asked early in a campaign that they are expected to consider the leadership gifts. These gifts are vital. They will ensure the success of your campaign and provide the momentum that is so very important in encouraging the rest of the congregation to give.

The reality for most church campaigns is that a handful of donors will give an amount equal to half or more of the financial goal. In almost all cases, 75 to 80 percent of all giving totals will come from 20 to 25 percent of the congregation. For campaigns with sizeable goals, as few as 5 to 10 percent of the donors will give an amount equal to 90 or 95 percent of the goal.

It is difficult to broadly determine how many people fall into the Advance Gifts category. That will depend upon your church and on how "advance gift" is defined. In general, anyone who has the capability of making a minimum gift of $3,000 to $5,000 or more over a three-year pledge payment period falls into what is called the "advance gift" category. Normally (but not always) 15 to 25 percent of a middle-class congregation can be counted on to pledge "advance gifts."

Advance Gifts Evaluation Meeting

Early in the Gifting Phase, the Advance Gifts Chair will preside over a key meeting called Advance Gifts Evaluation early in the Gifting Phase. This meeting is absolutely critical to the success of the program. The Advance Gifts Chair along with the rector (usually), the church treasurer, the campaign chair, and perhaps a few other parishioners of financial means meet to ascertain which people should be asked to consider a gift. This is a very confidential meeting. Some people feel uncomfortable about this part of the process, so church committees often avoid carrying out this crucial exercise. Because it is necessary for success, though, outside counsel will insist and ensure that leadership literally go through the church directory for this estimation exercise. The Advance Gifts Evaluation is based on the giving range estimated during the feasibility study, the prospect's annual stewardship gift, donations made to other organizations, and/or the perceived giving capacity of the prospect based on other information.

Following the Advance Gifts Evaluation meeting, a committee composed of major gift donors will be identified who will make the divisional calls. This process will be based on financial peers calling on financial peers; these matches must be made appropriately. For example, the $10,000 donor calls on persons in his or her giving range. The $1,000 donor does not call on the $10,000 prospect.

Why Is a Suggested Amount Necessary?

People need guidance in order to give the appropriate amount. Often they will ask the solicitor one or both of these questions: "How much did you give?" and/or "What do you want me to do?" The Advance Gifts evaluation is critical in this phase and provides the guidelines needed by volunteers, particularly the estimation of how much prospects can give. The solicitor should not simply go to people and ask, "Would you make a gift?" Rather, they should ask: "Would you consider a leadership gift?" referring the prospect to the Gifts Essential Chart in the materials. Or solicitors might ask one of these questions: "Would you consider joining me in the range of such and such?" or, "I am making a gift in the range of such and such. Would you consider the same giving level?"

This way of asking is important. Most people welcome the knowledge about what they should consider in order to accomplish the church goal. If you do not suggest a giving level, human nature will take over and people will give less than is going to be necessary to achieve success in your campaign. People want to do what is appropriate, and they look for guidance from the solicitor. The Advance Gift Committee members will learn how to make a solicitation during the Advance Gift Worker Training meeting.

Advance Gift Worker Training

During this phase, conduct the first worker training session for the major gifts. The worker training session is critical.

Basically, the agenda for worker orientation and training is as follows:

- Open with the campaign prayer.

- Premiere the campaign brochure. It is the tool the callers will use when meeting with a prospect.

- Describe the organization campaign plan and timeline.

- Inform the callers what is expected of them.

- Conduct role-playing exercises on "How to Ask for a Gift."

- Record the cards that each worker takes. (Ideally, they have been pre-assigned based on financial peer relationships.)

- Set dates, generally weekly, for workers to report on the success of their calls. These can be conference calls or e-mail communications.

Recording Gifts

As gifts are received, it is necessary to record them. The campaign clerical person records the pledges. The church treasurer or bookkeeper makes the deposits. A thank-you letter should go out as quickly as possible after the pledge or gift is made. This initial letter from the clerical person affirms the pledge arrangements; however, a personal, handwritten note of thanks should be sent to each donor by the rector and Campaign Chair and/or Advance Gifts Chair. Later, the clerical assistant will send reminder letters containing updates on the progress of the project. It is absolutely critical to track every pledge card. Failure to track pledge cards, to keep up with who has what card, is a recipe for disaster.

The Kick-Off Weekend

The Advance Gifts workers have been working for several weeks and gifts and pledges are on hand. Your campaign is now ready for the official kick-off weekend to launch the Congregational Gifts Division. This is an important and festive occasion involving the first kick-off event, and usually involving some type of meal. It is the "Great Coming Together." In physicists' terms, you are entering into "critical mass," in which you have to "explode" the campaign on the congregation.

The type of event you should hold will depend on the culture of your church. Some churches go to a big hotel or a country club for a dinner; others have a picnic on the grounds or a catered affair in the parish or fellowship hall. Whatever suits your culture, work very hard at this event and make it very special. Schedule musicians to perform—either members of the church or a special band you decide to hire. Invite former clergy who would appreciate the fellowship with their previous congregation. Try to have everybody there who has had a positive impact on the life of the church. Run special vans to pick up the elderly and shut-ins, and provide childcare services so young parents can attend. The highlight of the program is the announcement of the total Advance Gifts raised to date. Usually, this is 60 to 70 percent of the goal. This exciting announcement raises the sights and enthusiasm of the members.

Do not charge for this event. Some people think if they pay $25 or $50 for the dinner, they have made their gift to the campaign; do not fall into this trap. Allocate money in the campaign budget for this activity—you will get the money back many, many times over. If you fail to have a kick-off event, you will find it much more difficult to get people to give to the campaign. Many simply will not have the focus that they need, and the campaign will be just another ordinary fund drive in their busy lives rather than the important, special episode that heightens their awareness and interest in the project and the church.

The Congregational Gifts Division

During this next phase, the remaining members, and even friends, of the congregation are approached, sometimes one-on-one, sometimes in small group meetings or festive events. Generally in the Congregational Gifts Phase, we find 75 to 85 percent of a middle-class congregation will be capable of giving donations anywhere from $25 to as high as $3,000 or even more.

In most cases, workers will attend the Congregational Gifts Worker Orientation and Training Session to select their pledge cards, to learn more about the campaign, to receive their materials, and to be inspired to go forth and visit their fellow parishioners. This session occurs a few days either before or after Dedication Sunday and the Kick-Off Event.

Workers who have been recruited by the Congregational Gifts Chair will come to the Worker Training Meeting and learn how to call on their fellow parishioners. The number of workers is based on the Rule of Five; one worker takes five cards. For example, your church has 100 potential giving units, 20 of whom have fallen into the Advance Gifts category. Then 80 cards will be available in the next category. Eighty divided by five suggests a need for 16 workers. Always try to recruit a few more than needed because some people (as many as one-third or more) will not work their cards, or something will happen (for instance, prospects will be out of town) and the workers will be unable to accomplish their calls in a timely fashion.

The volunteers can select the prospects they wish to contact. Their job is much easier than the Advance Gifts callers since they are not asking for consideration of a specific amount to be donated. They are emissaries of the campaign and will personally deliver the campaign brochure and pledge card. During the visit, they can explain the projects, answer questions, and give guidance about how to complete the pledge card. When they are asked, "What do you want me to do?" they can refer the prospect to the Gifts Essential Chart. This way, they are giving guidance without asking for an amount. The fact that a parishioner is taking the time to deliver the materials is testimony to his or her belief in the importance of the campaign. A gift of time is a very special gift in and of itself, and the prospect will realize this.

Again, it is necessary to have scheduled reporting sessions to keep the solicitors motivated and on track. These can be done by conference calls, e-mail messages, and/or gatherings with the leadership, or whatever works in your church culture.

Alternative Methods

In this day when recruiting enough volunteers to make one-on-one calls is a challenge, an alternative solicitation method has worked successfully in some very large congregations as well as in small churches.

During the Congregational Gifting Phase, your church can schedule a series of events that are appropriate to the diversity of your congregation: a tea for the seniors, an after-church brunch for families (with entertainment for children during the program portion), an after-work gathering for the younger members, and so forth. These social events include a short program to introduce campaign leadership, review the campaign objectives and goal, and explain how to complete a pledge card. (Often a blow-up of the card is used to help illustrate the features). Then leaders direct people to go to a table, pick up their pledge card, and complete it in privacy. Provide an envelope for the card, as well as an attractive container in which the members may place their sealed envelopes.

With well-executed communication, people will know they can attend one or more events and complete their card there, rather than having someone visit them. Those who are committed to the campaign, as demonstrated in the feasibility study, will certainly find this a more appealing way to make their commitment. Following the events, determine which prospects still remain and devise the best method of solicitation for each—personal calls, telephoning, and/or direct mail.

Celebration and Acknowledgment

Schedule a concluding event. Plan a Sunday of Thanksgiving in which, through prayer, song, and spoken words, you announce the good news that additional ministry is enabled because of the generosity of the congregation in the effort just concluded. Recognize the volunteer leadership for their participation.

The number of weeks workers will need to make their calls will depend on the size of your congregation. Conduct weekly report meetings. As the reports come in, the campaign clerical person should send out the acknowledgments and letters signed by the appropriate campaign leadership. Gifts are recorded and deposited. The campaign comes to a formal end in terms of the solicitation, usually within four to five months.

Post-Campaign Review

Consider the appointment of an ongoing Post-Campaign Review Committee as the drive concludes. This committee should meet quarterly to evaluate how the pledge collection is proceeding, discover what the attrition rate is, and do what is necessary to encourage that attrition be held as low as possible.

Even after the campaign comes to a formal conclusion, regular communication is still necessary to tell people how wisely the church is using their funds over the life of the pledge pay-out period. For example, when the ground-breaking is scheduled, make sure that the entire church body is invited to the event, and ensure you have regular announcements in your bulletins and newsletters about the progress of the funded projects. To keep attrition at a minimum, communicate orally and in writing about how plans are proceeding.

If you are a medium-sized church of perhaps 100 to 300 giving unit prospects, the average time it should take to conduct your campaign from beginning to end is three to five months. It will take perhaps three to five years for all the pledges to be collected. Generally speaking, within the first year, you will receive 35 to 40 percent of all your gifts from the pledges. In year two, expect to receive 25 to 30 percent of your gift total, while in year three, you might receive only 20 to 25 percent. The remaining amount will trickle in during years four and five. Unfortunately, you should also expect some attrition, approximately 5 percent for the average church campaign. Several reasons can account for this, including people moving, passing away, getting angry with the church or its members, and transferring to other churches—these things just happen. The more efficient you can be in sending out reminder notices and celebrating the good works resulting from the generosity of the congregation, the more you can hold attrition to a minimum. You will also likely experience a rise in stewardship after the pledge payment period is over. People were used to making an extra gift to the campaign, and they often add this amount to their annual gifting once their pledge is complete. One rector in a northern state reported that stewardship increased 18 percent following the last year of the pledge payments.

SIX

Common Questions about a Church Capital Campaign

PEOPLE OFTEN ASK, "Can we go outside of the congregation to raise funds?" The short answer is usually no. The longer answer is "sometimes." Friends and church alumni, yes. Generally speaking, businesses, corporations, and most foundations cannot or will not give to religious causes.

If your church has a significant outreach program that serves the community, though, such as a daycare center or a school that serves the community, you may be able to present your church to the public as a community resource, especially if they are separate 501C3s. These programs and/or organizations may provide the leverage necessary to approach individuals, businesses, and foundations that would not normally give to a church cause.

We are reminded of a church in New York City that was, in essence, the community center for the neighborhood. Disadvantaged young people in the area used the center during the day and the homeless adults at night. It was a wonderful ministry, but the church was literally wearing out from constant use. It was necessary and prudent to include the community as well as the congregation in the church's capital campaign.

We caution that if you do go outside of a church, though, your campaign will probably take longer because you will have to create an organization and communication plan above and beyond the membership of the congregation. It may take longer, it may take more in terms of discernment, management time, and oversight, but the financial rewards usually are there. Be sure to consider people besides church members who might also help in your campaign. Extended families who have relatives buried in the church cemetery, for instance, might be willing to give to the campaign. There are members of what we might euphemistically call the "Church Alumni Society" that should be researched and approached, for example, retirees who have moved to another part of the country. Overturn all stones possible. If community organizations are using your building during the day or evening, you might approach these groups and ask for gifts, especially self-help groups that use the building on a regular basis.

Some older churches are on the National Register of Historical Places or a similar local or state list. There may be the possibility of government grants at the municipal, state, or federal levels to assist in maintaining physical structures, especially if the program has to do with physical restoration or historic preservation. Generally, these governmental bodies cannot assist churches with any type of program involving Christian education and worship, but they might be able to help you preserve the facade or integrity of the building. This is especially true in some of our larger cities where there may be an urban foundation or a local governmental unit that can be helpful.

Various foundations throughout the United States can assist in historic preservation of sacred spaces. Go online or to your local public library for names, interests, and addresses. Although looking into this *may* be beneficial, these grants are very difficult to obtain. It may be worth checking into if you are trying to preserve a historical structure. In one recent campaign, a church served as a national monument. Friends and groups outside of the congregation were encouraged to assist in the preservation of the building. The church was able to present itself to a larger public as a monument, eligible for corporate gifts and worthy of support from friends who would not normally give to church campaigns.

Explore all options, but for a suburban church, a church in a smaller town, or a church that does not have any type of community service that is of an outstanding nature, it is best to count on support only from those within the congregation.

What Should We Expect of the Congregation?

First, how do we define the membership of a church? This can vary from church to church, denomination to denomination. Generally speaking, the people on your mailing list comprise the membership. These are the people who receive the questionnaire mailed during the feasibility study. This is the body from which you *hope* to draw the majority of your financial strength during your campaign.

In most churches in most mainline denominations, only 50 to 70 percent of the family units considered members are giving regularly to the church either through a formal pledge or with regular contributions. Even though one may communicate regularly with the other 50, 40, or 30 percent of the church "membership," it is usually very difficult to involve them in a capital program.

One general rule is, "If people aren't giving regularly to the annual budget to support the ongoing ministry of the church, don't expect them to give to the campaign itself." This concept is very frustrating to clergy or lay committee chairs who know that certain members are owners of large businesses or have considerable wealth that could help to underwrite the church campaign but choose not to. Extremely wealthy people who do not give to the church on a regular basis but are claimed as members generally contribute to a campaign only when financial peers call on them and say something like, "I gave to your museum campaign last year. Would you join me in giving to our church?" This is disappointing, but it does not mean that these individuals are not generous. They may be financially generous throughout the community but not to or through the church.

In chapter two we profiled a typical Episcopal congregation. And while we hesitate to divide people into these categories and recognize that situations overlap, the following remains useful to an understanding of your congregation.

Giving Profile of a Congregation

Percentage of Congregation	Category	Expected Donation
10 to 20 percent	The Converted	Generous donors or tithers or those working toward the tithe, giving 3 to 10 percent of their income
35 to 50 percent	The Committed	1 to 3 percent of their income
30 to 45 percent	The Uncommitted	Little or nothing

The Converted

Denominations vary and churches within the denominations differ, but among the membership are people whom we shall call the Converted. They represent the 10 to 20 percent of the members who try to tithe or are tithing. They are extremely faithful and when they make a gift, they are not giving to the church, they are "giving to God." Most are on a spiritual journey and will be very supportive, to the extent that they can, of a capital campaign; however, some of these people are already "tapped out" because they are so generous on an annual basis.

The Committed

The next group of individuals is called the Committed. These are people who compose anywhere from 35 to 50 percent of the congregation. These folks give, but they generally do not tithe. They serve on leadership committees, and they attend church regularly. They are on a journey, but are not yet totally "converted." They are giving not necessarily to God but to the church.

This group can be demanding in what they expect of the church in terms of services. They want a Christian education program for the children and youth, the sermon to be well prepared, and the facilities to be attractive, functional, and clean, especially the restrooms and nursery. For their financial generosity, they expect value. If the church fails to deliver service or if there is conflict among top leadership, these individuals often go shopping for another church. They often have a consumer mentality. There is a great deal less loyalty to denominations than there has been in previous generations. The "committed" individuals are quicker to move from denomination to denomination in order to find a comfort level and value for their giving.

Yet these individuals are absolutely critical to a capital campaign. This is one reason to conduct extensive readiness activities, such as a feasibility study, and to prepare campaign brochures; many of these people have a high need for information. They want to be involved in the decision-making process. If these people are left out of the decision-making process, their giving will be low. This group is composed of opinion makers and very busy people who want to spend their time wisely and make sure their donations are thoughtfully used.

The Uncommitted

The third group, called the Uncommitted, may compose anywhere from 30 to 45 percent of the congregation. They are on the rolls and they receive the newsletter, but they do attend church services only on Christmas and Easter or perhaps for marriages and funerals. They do not give very much, if at all. They may place a twenty-dollar bill in the offering plate on Christmas Eve. This group may contain some extremely wealthy people who have no regular pattern of giving to the church, and yet they call themselves members of the congregation. Enlisting their help in any capital campaign is, more often than not, frustrating and disappointing.

The Length of a Campaign

How long does a church campaign last? One model indicates that church campaigns can last anywhere from three to five months, depending upon the size of the goal and congregation. While three to five months may be required for the act of solicitation alone, it usually takes three months to complete a feasibility study. In addition, you may spend several months, even years, in the discernment phase just to prepare for the feasibility study.

Many factors determine the length of the campaign, including the involvement of financial leadership, the season of the year, the need for increased public relations within the congregation, the informing of major gift prospects, and the size of the goal. You certainly shouldn't rush through the campaign, as many contributions are missed in a compressed effort. Leadership gifts may be smaller than they could have been because of the failure to adequately inform and enthusiastically involve all prospects.

The Campaign Season

What is the best time of the year to do the campaign? Traditionally, campaigns have been held from late August to mid-December and from January on to June. However, recent experience indicates that it is possible to hold campaigns during the summer. It may take a little bit longer because more people are on vacation, but it is not always a bad time of the year, especially for summer chapels. The kick-off event can be a Fourth of July picnic or some other kind of outdoor activity. American life is extremely busy, and there is no perfect time of the year anymore. Also remember, tax advantages usually are not what encourage one to give to a church capital campaign, so don't rush a December program to catch year-end giving if the parish is not ready.

The Capital Drive and Annual Stewardship

Someone is bound to ask, "Can we conduct a capital campaign at the same time as the annual stewardship drive?" Many would say no. The realistic answer is yes. We've already mentioned how busy church members can be. What a wonderful opportunity it would be to support the ministry of the church by asking people to contribute to both the annual stewardship drive and the capital campaign.

During the solicitation, some members will inevitably say that they can't give to both efforts; you shouldn't push them for the capital campaign gift. The annual stewardship effort must always come first. If you're considering doing your capital campaign at the same time as you do your stewardship drive, be sure to ask about the viability of this in the feasibility study. This puts people on alert. If workers are trained properly and if a communication plan is executed, a church can accomplish both activities at the same time. Volunteers will appreciate the savings in time. Our experience has been that annual stewardship can actually increase during a capital drive. The workers are trained, organized, and encouraged to make those important one-on-one calls and share more complete stewardship information.

Building Endowment

Can gifts for the endowment be raised at the same time as funds for brick and mortar? Yes. Many campaigns involve meeting restoration needs as well as raising money for the endowment. One church in the Midwest raised endowment funds to underwrite a full-time Christian education director. Four years later we were called back to help plan for classroom expansion due to the success of the program!

How do you raise endowment? First, ask directly for pledges over a multi-year period. Second, engage in a planned giving program, which is the encouragement of bequest in wills and life income gifts such as charitable gift annuities and trusts.

Can a church conduct planned giving programs and endowment drives at the same time as a brick-and-mortar capital campaign? As long as people are focused on the ministry of the church, we've found that churches can conduct these campaigns simultaneously. On a number of occasions, even during the feasibility study process, we have identified and helped create planned gifts, such as charitable remainder trusts or real estate donations.

We hasten to add, however, that the endowment effort, begun as part of focused attention during your capital drive, is merely the beginning. Planned giving marketing should occur quarterly, year after year, to encourage people to remember the church in their estate plans. If done properly, a church can have a successful capital drive, a successful annual stewardship effort, and make a significant beginning in building endowment.

Raising money in a capital campaign, though, is a little like playing a hand of bridge. Whether one is bidding six no-trump or two diamonds, it is going to take the same thoughtful effort. The same is true with a capital program; certain activities have to occur no matter the size of the goal. Generally speaking, the larger the goal, the less expensive it is on a percentage basis to provide the management oversight and communications necessary to achieve the level of success you would like to have.

A Sample Budget

The sample budget for your campaign should include the following items:

- the management fee to the firm that is providing the service for your campaign to include travel, meals, and lodging for the consultant (Be wary of firms that charge a percentage of the goal achieved, which can encourage high-pressure tactics and dubious gift reporting.)
- clerical support
- office equipment including computers, printers, copiers, fax machines, and telephones with messaging capabilities
- office supplies
- meal meetings
- kick-off event
- telephone and e-mail
- campaign materials—brochures, pledge cards, etc.
- postage
- contingencies
- awards and honorariums

Do You Need Capital Campaign Counsel?

Regardless of the size of your goal, you may wish to consider contracting with a campaign management firm that has conducted church capital drives. Even relatively small campaigns can benefit from outside counsel, at least for the preparation of a fund-raising plan (including a timeline, job descriptions for the tasks of leadership, worker orientation and training, and the production of brochures and materials).

The level of appropriate management oversight needed varies from church to church depending on the availability of leadership, the complexity of the project, and the size of the goal and congregation. Statistics indicate that campaigns that do not use professional counsel raise one-quarter to one-half less than those that do.

What Should You Expect from Outside Counsel?

Think of your outside counsel as the producer or director of a play in which the volunteers are the main actors. The necessary preparation to put on a play is done by your campaign counsel. Don't expect your counsel to solicit gifts; this rarely happens. The solicitation of gifts is a one-on-one activity conducted by volunteers, clergy leadership, and financial peers.

Expect your counsel to:

- Organize your campaign calendar.

- Create job descriptions for leadership.

- Assist in identifying and evaluating advance gift prospects.

- Coordinate the writing and production of materials.

- Assist planning for events such as kick-off dinners and closing celebrations.

- Provide orientation, ongoing training, and leadership.

- Ensure that the communications plan is being executed.

- Provide both strategic and tactical advice.

- Ensure gifts are properly recorded and acknowledged.

Outside counsel will set deadlines for you, force you to do the appropriate evaluations, and ensure, to the greatest extent possible, that you will do one-on-one calls. In short, your counsel provides the game plan and discipline to ensure success.

There are other reasons to consider outside counsel. By hiring counsel, you are essentially hiring time. Americans can easily be described as "over-scheduled." Yet what is required is time to manage the complex task of going from zero revenue to several hundred thousand, perhaps several million dollars, in a relatively short period of time. Someone has to write and execute the plan, see that deadlines are met, and manage the office to make sure appropriate communication occurs. When you bring in outside counsel, you can be assured that those activities are going to be carried out as effectively and efficiently as possible.

You are also hiring expertise. You are bringing in someone who is trained and has the experience to execute a methodology that has worked well in church after church. A variety of methodologies have proven very effective. Some consulting firms stress certain nuances; other firms emphasize different techniques. Basically, though, the process involves getting people organized, sharing information, and executing the plan with a sense of ministry, not high-pressure tactics.

Check to be sure that the person you hire has all the organizational "people skills" necessary to take the project from start to finish in a short period of time. Ask for references from previous campaigns.

"Fund raising" conjures up all sorts of concepts. There is nothing mysterious about it; it is essentially the process of creating and executing a management and communication plan. It takes time, involves many people, and requires a great deal of information sharing. What you should expect when you bring someone in from the outside is insurance that all the nuts and bolts are put in place and that nothing will fall through the cracks. The investment you make in outside management, for whatever period of time, will help you to have a much more efficient and effective campaign. If you try to do it yourself, you may find you are not efficient enough in encouraging people to maximize their giving potential; you may not be prepared for scheduled meetings. You may lack the discipline to see that the cards are worked so that the campaign will end on time. Volunteers likely will not be as committed to each other as they would be to paid expertise.

The inevitable question is, "If we use an outside consulting firm, how much will it cost?" Fees vary depending on the length of service time, the expertise, the location of the firm, and your location. Generally speaking, daily fees are about the same you would pay an attorney, a CPA, or other professional advisor. There may be travel costs associated with the fee, either in addition to the professional fee or included in it. Be sure you have a written understanding of how time and expenses will be billed.

How much outside consulting service is necessary? You should use only the amount needed to accomplish your task. Again, this amount varies, as some firms place a manager on site continuously for a number of weeks or a number of months, while others promote "in-and-out" service, limiting the days of consulting. Fax machines and e-mail make it a lot easier for consultants to be off-site these days. And thanks to airplanes, no church, church school, or agency is more than a few hours away from a consultant. For smaller campaigns, the church might seek a mentoring relationship. Whatever your needs, it is possible, even with the smallest campaign, to use a consultant in a way that is both economical and effective.

SEVEN

How to Prepare for and Execute a Diocese-wide Capital Campaign

"Where there is no vision, the people perish." —Proverbs 29:18 (KJV)

AT TIMES, CAPITAL CAMPAIGNS extend beyond individual parishes. Church agencies, college chaplaincies, seminaries, and other organizations may need to raise funds on occasion. To develop a successful effort that involves many churches working toward a common goal of advancing mutual ministries, you must understand the dynamics involved. For the sake of simplicity, let us examine the preparation necessary for a diocesan campaign in the Episcopal Church. The lessons provided and the methodologies described are similar to all extensive regional and national denominational efforts.

The Diocesan Campaign

Conducting a diocese-wide capital campaign is a time-consuming, challenging effort for the bishop and diocesan leadership and should not be undertaken lightly. Much prayer, soul-searching, visioning, and communicating must occur if a bishop is to lead a diocese in a successful effort. Just as in a church campaign, diocesan leadership should consider a capital drive effort in three major phases:

1. Discernment
2. Feasibility Study
3. Gifting

The first recorded religious capital campaign is described in Exodus 35 and 36. It was easy (or so it seems by hindsight) for Moses to know the will of God, as God personally challenged Moses and Aaron to build a tabernacle in the wilderness. People gave so joyfully that Moses had to command the donors to quit giving! This is the first, and probably the last, campaign in which leadership had to tell people *not* to give more.

Discerning the will of God is not as easy for most modern-day bishops as it was for Moses. Leadership may have a vision of enhanced ministry that requires financial resources, but for most dioceses and church agencies, communicating the vision and seeking to know the will of the Almighty is a process and not an instant revelation.

Every diocese must involve laypersons and clergy in the visioning and discernment process. Too frequently, leaders have to stop in the middle of a campaign to explain the purposes and goals of the diocesan fund drive, only to discover that the laity and clergy aren't at all invested in the campaign.

Discernment

People tend to support and contribute more readily to causes when they are involved in the development of the campaign objectives. This is true of clergy as well as laity. Both must prayerfully discern for themselves what God is calling the church and people to accomplish. If people are not aware a campaign is going to occur, they cannot plan to give to it, so you must continuously communicate the needs and visions to everyone involved.

It is normal for local clergy and laity to feel financially threatened when the diocese or a church charity or school considers raising funds by approaching members of the congregation directly. Sharing the vision and explaining how the campaign would unfold helps to reduce anxiety, encourages cooperation, and can produce early consideration of giving.

Clergy and other leadership need to realize that although many church members are already giving generously to local community capital campaigns, many will respond to a diocesan vision if an urgent and compelling cause is shared. A diocese-wide campaign does not reduce the annual giving potential of a congregation; eventually the opposite occurs. People become comfortable with giving at higher levels and often pass this generosity along in future years to the local church.

When church leaders are involved early in the planning process, many begin to think about their own local needs. This is especially true in a diocesan campaign. A sizeable percentage of churches will elect to embark on their own campaigns during the diocesan effort. In part this occurs because the diocese dared to share a vision, set a calendar, and enforce deadlines. A local endeavor, while somewhat reducing the potential for diocesan gifts, develops financial resources for other vital ministries that, in turn, ultimately strengthen the diocese.

If planned giving is to be a part of a diocesan effort to build endowment, consider inviting churches to join in establishing a common goal for planned giving (wills, charitable trusts, real estate, and other gifts) at the local level.

Work in Partnership

Leadership might ask churches to join in a partnership for ministry development. Local leadership is more likely to embrace the proposed campaign with enthusiasm if they perceive that the diocese is reaching out to help all parts of the church in financial development and that their local congregation will benefit from the effort. A consultant can work individually with churches, reviewing the possibilities of strengthening both parish and diocesan ministries through strong co-capital campaigns, annual steward-ship, and planned giving initiatives.

We call this partnership approach CAP (CAPITAL, ANNUAL GIVING, AND PLANNED GIVING). While not neglecting the potential of large individual giv-ing, we have discovered a tremendous increase in participation in the diocese-wide effort if we are able to assist local churches in addressing their own financial and ministry needs. Local churches are then asked to tithe to the diocesan effort from their own effort. When readiness activities are properly done, the feasibility study will reveal more enthusiasm, higher possible gift levels, additional names of leadership, more cooperation from clergy and lay leaders, and the real possibility of strengthening both local and diocesan min-istries, increasing the success of the campaign.

Conducting Discernment Activities

Organizing and communicating in geographical areas the size of a diocese, with numerous churches, is always challenging. This step-by-step method will engage the leadership and provide clergy and lay people alike with a vision for ministry.

1. Generally, a bishop and a few diocesan leaders begin to perceive the need for funds for enhanced ministries in the diocese. These thoughts are usually shared first with diocesan council or the diocesan execu-tive committee. The council may appoint an exploratory capital cam-paign committee to draft a vision statement. The appointment of a committee is announced in diocesan publications. The committee is composed of lay and clergy opinion makers, persons who share a pas-sion for certain ministries. Ideally some of those on the committee are also philanthropic leaders.

2. The committee drafts the first statement outlining possible projects to be funded.

3. The bishop and other diocesan leaders, both clergy and lay, begin shar-ing the vision, asking for prayers and feedback.

4. The leadership then organizes clergy and lay conferences, at which a consultant can explain in detail how a diocesan campaign would work. Attendees break into small groups, study the vision, and report back to a facilitator. The proposed projects continue to be refined and per-haps added to as feedback is received.

5. The bishop asks the faithful to pray about what they may be called to do in response to the vision, as well as respond to their own calling to preach the gospel and build the church. Clergy ask their congregations to examine their own ministry-enhancement opportunities and to join in a visioning process.

6. The revised vision is taken to additional area meetings where it can be shared with clergy, members of diocesan committees, congregational leaders, and delegates to the next diocesan convention. Feedback is encouraged. Leadership can challenge the churches to consider their possible "Partnership in Ministry," or CAP participation. It is important to begin and end these sessions with Scripture and prayer, as this process is a true search for the voice of God.

7. The outcome of all these activities is communicated through the diocesan newspaper, by special letters, on the website, in any in-house newsletters, and by e-mail to clergy and lay leaders.

8. The bishop, clergy, and lay leadership meet with as many local church leaders and major donor prospects as possible. Begin searching for key philanthropic leadership, both clergy and lay, to direct the campaign. Historically, wealthy people have helped to build the church and enable ministry, so do not be reluctant to involve people of financial means in this cause. They too need to be encouraged to give and lead through the spiritual interaction that comes from conversation and challenge by a bishop or clergy person. Small group meetings and one-on-one sessions with people of means during discernment are crucial.

9. The Exploratory Committee refines the vision and returns it to the diocesan council. Following endorsement, it is presented at the diocesan convention, where all congregations are represented. Each part of the proposed program should be thoroughly examined during the convention, often in committee. Give people the opportunity to ask questions. Challenge members to to pray, study, discern, vision, and reason together.

From this convention may come a resolution to conduct a feasibility study. At this juncture, an outside consulting firm is usually employed to prepare an objective evaluation. A survey will take several months. The bishop and council may be authorized to launch a campaign if the study is positive, or the convention may ask for a specially called session to study the results of the survey and vote whether or not to proceed.

Continue to disseminate information throughout this process. Every member of the church is continuously asked to give to many worthy causes. A diocesan campaign may be a "holy endeavor," but it too requires the use of every communication skill and organizational method available.

Why Feasibility Study?

The bishop and leadership may have a vision and believe that they are responding to God's will, but there also comes a time when they must know the will of the clergy and lay leadership. The formal survey to explore the feelings of the diocese is known as the feasibility study.

A diocesan feasibility study seeks to ascertain the following:

- Do clergy and laity support the proposed projects?

- Which projects have priority?

- What projects omitted from the proposed plans should be included?

- Are clergy and laity willing to volunteer their time and talents?

- Are they willing to make gifts?

- Do sizeable leadership gifts exist?

- Are new leadership gift prospects suggested?

- Would people consider planned giving?

- What financial goal is appropriate? Can it be attained?

- Which churches are considering their own capital campaigns?

- Which churches could benefit from assistance to strengthen annual stewardship and planned giving/endowment ventures through the CAP program?

- Are there competing community and church agency capital campaigns?

- Is the suggested timing appropriate?

- Will the economy support a campaign during the suggested time frame?

A formal study may take two to four months to complete. Materials have to be prepared; people must be interviewed or sent a questionnaire by mail. All clergy and lay leaders (diocesan and local) should express their opinions formally. Leadership gift prospects should be surveyed in person.

Positive studies do not automatically commit dioceses to campaigns. In our firm, on a number of occasions, a strong discernment process has suggested a delay or revision of the goal and objectives. The study also allows the diocese to work closely with the selected consulting firm to determine if the company performs appropriately and if the chemistry is good between the leadership and the consultants. The feasibility study will determine if the firm has the skills to assist churches in strengthening their programs simultaneously through co-capital drives, annual stewardship assistance, and planned giving.

After the Feasibility Study, Share the News!

Assuming the study is positive, it is now time to prepare for the campaign. Share the results of the study throughout the diocese through the diocesan newsletter, websites, e-mail, the spoken word, clergy conferences, council and convention meetings, and key leadership meetings. Usually the diocesan convention is the appropriate place for membership to vote on moving forward. Use this occasion to celebrate the expected increase in mission and ministry. Urge all involved to share the Good News of God in Christ, to take this opportunity to go forth with enthusiasm and encourage others in their support of enhancing the church's mission.

Directing the Diocesan Campaign

Recruit leadership, communicate, organize, and ask people to join in giving.

Depending on the location and size of the diocese and the readiness of all churches to participate, a campaign may take nine to eighteen months or longer if the CAP program is adopted. The bishop, clergy, and lay leadership must set aside time for asking for gifts. If a full-blown partnership in ministry program stressing co-church campaigns is envisioned, the effort may become an initiative and take several years to reach maturity.

Usually leadership will divide a diocesan campaign into two major phases. A quiet Advance Gifts Phase occurs in which major donor prospects are informed, visited, and asked for their financial participation. Diocesan leadership works very closely with local parishes during this phase to ensure cooperation. After the Advance Gifts Phase, with a considerable portion of the pledges and donations in hand, diocesan leadership officially kicks off the campaign with a central event, such as a diocese-wide dinner, and proclaims a Dedication Sunday throughout the diocese.

Next, during the Congregational Phase, volunteers in local churches call on their fellow members to join in giving to the diocesan effort, or people make their gifts privately at special events. From the beginning of the effort, and in some cases for years, a consultant may work with individual parishes to prepare for co-campaigns, more effective annual stewardship drives, or establishing planned giving programs (CAP). Churches, as part of their participation in the program, may elect to tithe or dedicate a larger percentage to the diocesan effort from this increase in financial resources.

During these months, instead of "business as usual," you have a wonderful opportunity to harvest gifts for ministry. Without resources, the church is less than it can be. With resources, the church can more fully share the gospel of Jesus Christ with a world in desperate need of the hope and grace of our Creator. Go forth to love and serve the Lord!

How Much Can Be Raised?

Generally speaking, the larger the diocese in terms of membership, the more funds you should be able to raise. Research indicates that in the 1990s (and our experience is similar) the average diocesan campaign raised approximately 2.5 million dollars. Some dioceses raised less, some much more. And this does not count the funds parishes may have raised in co-campaigns. Of course, in addition to membership size, there are many other variables that affect the diocesan outcome, such as:

- the state of the regional economy

- any diocesan or theological issues that may divide the church

- a lack of philanthropic leaders aligned with the diocese or church

- large churches having their own major capital campaigns, thus reducing diocesan potential

- diocesan leadership's level of commitment to the effort

Our firm, through the CAP Program, has assisted parishes in raising tens of millions of dollars for local needs as the diocese gathers its own resources. In such cases, ministries, programs, and properties have been greatly expanded, benefiting all parts of the church. Your diocese can do the same!

EIGHT

How to Prepare for a Church School Capital Campaign

To THIS POINT, we have examined how to prepare for and conduct church and diocesan capital campaigns. Church schools—by which we mean schools independent of government ownership, attached to or formally sponsored by a congregation or denomination—have similar financial needs. The num ber of church schools has grown significantly in recent decades in the United States. In the Episcopal Church, there are approximately 1,100 preschools and schools, or one for every seven churches. While financially underwritten by tuition, few schools could survive without annual giving support from church sponsors, parents, grandparents, friends, and alumni.

Discernment

As with a church or denominational capital campaign, positioning a church school for a capital drive is as important as conducting the funds drive itself. To maximize your school's potential for soliciting and receiving needed financial resources, carefully consider the following steps as the part of the discernment phase:

1. Identify the needs of the school.
2. Identify the constituency.
3. Involve the constituency.
4. Inform the constituency.

The points on the "wheel of fortune" in chapter one will also come in handy when preparing for a church school fund drive.

Identify the Needs of the School

Why is the school leadership considering a capital improvement program? Do you need to expand by adding a chapel, classrooms, a lunchroom, library, laboratories, or gymnasium? Is the school in need of remodeling or atten-dance to deferred maintenance?

Appoint an Exploratory Committee to meet with an architect or con-tractor if maintenance or construction is the aim of your program. The com-mittee should tour the facilities and make recommendations. Involve teachers or staff who use or will use the facilities; their input is valuable. Consider appointing senior students, parents and grandparents of students, alumni, and influential or helpful members of the community to this committee. In addition to bringing fresh ideas to the process, these members will help to interpret the project to the constituencies they represent. You can also visit other schools and examine how they have handled similar needs.

Matters of church-related schools require close cooperation with the clergy and official leadership of the church. A church school may need formal church approval before engaging in a campaign. Follow the guidelines, either formal or informal, appropriate to the situation. Appoint church representatives to serve as liaisons to your Exploratory Committee.

In many cases, the church and school share space, so the school campaign will actually be a joint church/school program. There are many challenges when two institutions with different missions share common ground and space. Purposeful listening is required, and working together joyfully is the key to a successful effort.

Your architect is a critical part of the team and must be experienced in school design. It is important to discuss fees in advance and to describe your vision as completely as possible.

Working with an architect, your Exploratory Committee should prepare and present first plans to the board (and vestry, if appropriate). After the plans are reviewed, it's time to broadcast the vision to the school's constituencies. This leads to our next major point on the "wheel of fortune."

Identify the Constituency

Who will make the gifts that are essential to ensure the success of your capital drive? Ideally, your school already has a strong annual giving program that benefits from the ongoing support of parents of current students, the board, and alumni.

Also consider these sources:

- grandparents and other relatives of students

- parents of former students

- members of the sponsoring church

- the larger local community (sometimes called "friends of the school")

- local philanthropists known to support education

- foundations and businesses

You might appoint a communications chair and committee at this point of your effort to insure that the planning message is being communicated as needed.

Involve Your Constituency

It is critical to invite feedback from opinion makers and philanthropic leaders. In your community, narrowcast to those major donor prospects and those who can influence opinions. Give those two groups as much ownership in the effort as possible. Schedule one-on-one sessions with them as well as small group meetings to share the vision and invite feedback. Remember, 80 percent or more of your total gifts will come from 20 percent or fewer of your donors. You must give special attention early and often to major donor prospects. Failure to do so risks failure of the campaign.

Inform Your Constituency

Devise a communication plan for each group. Plans may include the following:

- newsletters
- special letters to parents
- bulletin inserts (for the church)
- alumni magazines
- websites and e-mail
- open house
- group tours
- private in-home meetings
- parents' day/night
- grandparents' day
- Chamber of Commerce–sponsored events
- stories and announcements in the media
- luncheons
- lobby displays
- speeches to local civic groups
- regular reports to your sponsoring church and religious denomination

Tell your story in as many ways and as often as possible. A strong public relations program will not only attract financial support but also new students.

Conduct a Feasibility Study

At the appropriate time, a key part of your communication is the feasibility study. An outside consultant or firm should systematically survey your constituencies to answer such fundamental questions as these:

1. Are your constituents supportive of the project?
2. Is the proposed campaign timing appropriate?
3. Are leadership gifts available?
4. Can the proposed financial goal be attained?
5. Is leadership available and willing to serve?
6. Is the sponsoring church supportive?

This study provides critical research necessary before launching your effort. You may find that you have to downsize your project if it is too ambitious for the financial potential of your prospects, or you may be forced to postpone the project if the timing is wrong due to, for example, competing community campaigns or a weak economy.

If the data is positive, you can now report back to the board and sponsoring church with the study. Fine tune your financial plans, including any necessary borrowing. You can move forward with confidence because you have:

- Correctly identified and responded to your school's needs.

- Identified the individuals and groups necessary for the financial success of this effort.

- Fully informed these individuals about your school and plans.

- Formally sought their opinions about the project and have acted on that information (perhaps modifying financial goals, plans, or timing).

If you have thoughtfully and carefully engaged in the above discernment, or readiness, activities, then you can enthusiastically launch your campaign and prepare to be of greater service to your students, the community, and the church you serve.

A Few Observations

Traditionally, only 15 to 20 percent of the school's students are associated with the sponsoring church. School leadership is often disappointed to learn in the study that many parents are not willing to donate to the church school campaign because they feel that they're already doing enough by paying tuition and participating in the annual giving program with their time and finances.

For this chapter, the key word is "church," because it identifies the unique-
ness of the school, and more often than not the church and school conduct
the campaign together. Many times both institutions share facilities and seek
to increase and improve physical space. Because such close ties exist between
a church and a church school, the participation of church members and their
willingness to give is critical. Often parents of school children are young and
lack the ability to make major gifts. Without the participation of the sponsoring church, the gift total may be minimal.

The Church School Campaign: The Gifting Phase

As you would for the church and area-wide church capital campaigns, divide
your school campaign into these phases:

- Organization

- Leadership Recruitment

- Advance Gifts

- General Gifts

- Celebration and Acknowledgment

A church school normally has a larger, more diverse constituency than a
church. The campaign may take longer and require more organization
because you need to coordinate and communicate with more groups. If there
is a significant alumni group, travel may be involved, possibly lengthening
the campaign but providing more prospects for donations.

The National Association of Episcopal Schools
Within the Episcopal Church, schools are blessed with a tremendous
resource, the National Association of Episcopal Schools, or NAES. Located
at Church Center, 815 Second Avenue in New York, this well-staffed organization is supervised by a board composed of school heads and trustees. It
offers a multitude of services, with programs ranging from assistance with
school start-ups and school leadership and chaplaincy deployment to conflict resolution and long-range planning. If your school is not a member of
this association, join immediately!

NINE
How to Prepare for a Church Agency Capital Campaign

MOST CHURCH AGENCIES or charities undertake capital campaigns only once every five or ten years. Planning and preparation alone takes months, even years, and involves dozens of people.

Remember these basic principles, regardless of the type of capital campaign:

1. People give to people. The most effective way to solicit a pledge is face-to-face personal contact. Committed individuals should visit their peers and state their purpose: "I believe in this cause. I am supporting it financially and personally. Will you join me in considering a gift?"
2. People give to urgent and compelling causes. They do not give to causes that seem unimportant to them, that are poorly planned or managed, or that are ineffectively communicated.
3. People will donate time and money to campaigns when they have been invited to provide input and advice. Volunteers and prospective donors should feel that they have ownership of a campaign. People effectively support campaigns when they have the opportunity to participate in the decision-making process.
4. People do not tend to support campaigns for agencies that are not financially stable. People give to success, not to "save" a failing agency.

The following steps explore the fundamental readiness, or discernment, activities necessary to help position a church agency to launch a successful capital campaign. These steps may be modified depending upon your organization's particular situation.

Assess Your Level of Readiness

None of us would build a house without drawing plans and laying a sure foundation. The same principles are true for any capital campaign.

Study closely the following template, which is designed to examine your organization's current state of readiness and provide specific goals to work toward. Honestly examine your agency's readiness posture, and be prepared to address concerns. A former vice president of our firm, Susan Stuart, devised the following helpful questions and responses.

Is Your Church Agency Ready for a Capital Campaign?

Each of the following sections details an integral part of your campaign. You can broadly establish the readiness of your organization by determining which of every three statements fits your situation best. Use the following list as a key:

1. If the first statement best defines your situation, you are ready to undertake a campaign.
2. If the second statement best defines your situation, you could soon be ready with more preparation.
3. If the third statement best defines your situation, you should consider delaying your campaign until the circumstances are resolved.

The Need

1. The organization has identified specific and urgent needs.
2. The organization is in the process of identifying specific and urgent needs.
3. The organization must still come to consensus on priority needs.

The Case

1. The organization has developed and written a compelling case explaining the campaign goals.
2. The organization is developing a compelling case.
3. The organization has not developed a compelling case.

The Board

1. The Board of Directors understands and embraces the long-term commitment of time and resources required for a successful campaign, and recognizes that fund raising is not only their responsibility but also a top priority.
2. The Board of Directors is willing to learn more about the personal commitment and financial investment required, as well as how to solicit gifts from their peers.
3. The Board of Directors has a limited ability to make commitments, provide leadership, or is still working to overcome its discomfort with solicitation and/or making financial donations.

Relationship

1. Board members and key volunteers have existing peer relationships with philanthropic leaders, church leaders, and major donors.
2. Board members and key volunteers have access to philanthropic leaders, major donors, and major gift prospects.

3. There are few or no relationships with church, philanthropic, and community leaders.

Communication
1. The organization communicates often (more than five times a year) with its donors, constituents, and prospects using newsletters, e-mail, websites, and other public relations tools.
2. The organization communicates occasionally (two to four times per year) with its donor base by newsletters, group meetings, occasional visits, and church talks, and through media outlets.
3. The organization does not have a public relations plan and communicates infrequently with its constituency.

The Budget
1. The project budget is as accurate as it possibly can be at this point in the planning process.
2. The project budget is an estimate provided by professionals.
3. The project requires more accurate financial projections before a budget can be shared.

Leadership
1. Articulate, enthusiastic individuals are available to lead and to share the vision.
2. Articulate, enthusiastic individuals are available on a limited basis.
3. No one is available to lead, make decisions, or share the vision with the community.

The Staff
1. The staff understands and supports the need for a campaign.
2. The staff is being educated about the need for a campaign.
3. The staff is not aware that a campaign is being considered.

The Community
1. All other funding opportunities have been examined before turning to the denomination and community at large for support.
2. Other funding opportunities are being explored.
3. Sources of financial support are not aware of the organization's needs.

It is imperative to communicate with potential donors and to build a base of philanthropic leadership. Failure to do so will delay your campaign and reduce your potential to receive gifts.

Preparing for a capital campaign also provides an opportunity to conduct an organizational self-assessment. Your organization may benefit from an evaluation of its governance, planning, marketing, fiscal management, personnel management, and other aspects of internal and external operations, including its relationship to sponsoring churches. Examining an organization's strengths and weaknesses in these areas educates those involved in the process and may reveal opportunities to better position the organization for future challenges.

The most common reasons for conducting a campaign revolve around constructing new buildings or remodeling existing ones, although extraordinary leaps in programming and endowment may also inspire campaigns. Your Board of Directors will appoint a committee, sometimes called a Needs Assessment Committee, to articulate how a campaign will enable the organization to better serve its mission. Most often, this takes the form of evaluating current and future needs, considering challenges and opportunities, and formalizing a case statement.

The organization's leadership should establish preliminary and final report dates and a written outline of the information required. Since the report will include recommendations for strategic action, include volunteers with a sense of vision and mission in this group. Make sure you set aside an appropriate block of time for meetings with the board to allow for full discussion and, if needed, revision of the plan.

If your community has a Capital Campaign Review Board, be sure to educate them about potential projects and ask them about reporting and scheduling guidelines. If your agency receives United Way funding, you also may need the approval of their Campaign Review Board before launching a campaign. The sponsoring church or churches or denomination may need to give their permission and/or endorsement as well.

Create a Framework to Support the Project

After the board has voted on the report of the Needs Assessment Committee, it is time to define the project in more detail. In a capital project, several task forces should be created to act simultaneously. Work may include: screening architects and builders, working with bankers about financing options, meeting with real estate agents, interviewing professional fund-raising counsel, and developing a preliminary budget. Your organization's size and tradition will determine how best to delegate these responsibilities. Be sure that the individuals or committees assigned to study options and deal with issues clearly understand the tasks they are being asked to complete. Keep in mind the importance of setting deadlines.

Share the News and Invite Input

After you select an architect, commission a draft plan with estimated costs for approval by your leadership. Share the building plans with as many of your constituents as possible. Print newsletter articles and hold cottage meetings and receptions to invite feedback. If the proposed project is sizeable, consider constructing and displaying a model in an appropriate place. Pay special attention to potential major donors. Keep the sponsoring church or denomination involved and informed every step of the way.

Find creative ways to continuously inform and involve your organization's key volunteers, staff, and constituents. Liberally delegate tasks to as many people as possible. While this may take some extra time, the benefits of sharing your enthusiasm for the project, asking for assistance, and including many people in the process should more than compensate.

Don't overlook a thoughtful, well-timed public relations effort. You can begin with low-key information sharing and build to coincide with major capital campaign activities. Most organizations do not communicate enough with their prospective donors.

Authorize a Feasibility Study

As with the church, area-wide church, or church school campaign, the agency's financial potential usually cannot be determined accurately without a thorough feasibility study. Conduct personal interviews with key leadership and potential major donors as well as a mail survey to your constituency. This two-track approach informs a large number of supporters about the organization's intentions, helps to establish an achievable financial goal for the campaign, and invites feedback and involvement.

Once completed, a good feasibility study will answer the following questions for a church agency:

1. Are the organization's key volunteers and major donors supportive of the plans as proposed?
2. Will the larger civic and philanthropic community support a campaign?
3. Is the sponsoring church and denomination supportive?
4. What are the priorities as seen by the general constituency?
5. Are people willing to give to the proposed capital campaign?
6. Have potential leadership gifts been identified?
7. Is the financial goal attainable, or does it need to be modified?
8. Is the proposed timing for the campaign appropriate; are there competing local campaigns, is the economy weak, etc.?
9. What additional information should be shared?

10. Who should chair the campaign and who should serve on the various committees?
11. Can the organization raise funds through planned gifts such as bequests in wills, gifts of appreciated stock, real estate, charitable trusts, and/or life insurance, or in-kind gifts?

As noted in earlier chapters, a feasibility study helps to clarify the vision that will become the focal point of the campaign. It can uncover concerns or problems and identify campaign volunteers and potential donations and type of gifts (in-kind, planned, or cash pledges). It is a vital investment in the success of any future capital drive effort.

Campaign Decisions Are Made

If the feasibility study is positive, the Board of Directors and key volunteer leaders should make the final decision on the size, scope, and timing of the campaign. Sometimes the dream is too ambitious and plans must be revised. It will take time to review and decide how to fine tune the plans and financial objectives. This process must be completed before you launch your drive.

Final Thoughts before the Campaign

The unique challenges of a campaign can spark fresh opportunities to fulfill the mission, make friends for the organization, and renew the dedication and spirit of current volunteers and staff. As with any process, there are peaks and valleys; however, with proper planning, wise execution, a strong commitment to attracting and involving philanthropic and church leadership, and an urgent and compelling case, you will succeed.

TEN

How to Raise Funds for Your College Chaplaincy

IN LATE 1996, the Reverend Gurdon Brewster, long-time chaplain at Cornell University in Ithaca, New York, approached our firm and asked if we could be of assistance in helping Episcopal college chaplaincies find greater financial resources for ministry. Chaplain Brewster and other leaders in the Episcopal Society for Ministry in Higher Education (ESMHE) were in discussions with the Episcopal Church Foundation and its executive director, Bill Andersen, seeking a grant for the training of college chaplaincies in development and fund raising. Brewster, building on a positive experience of raising funds for the Cornell Chaplaincy Endowment, sought to encourage other Episcopal college chaplaincies to seek their own additional resources for their ministries.

Although our firm had extensive experience with Episcopal parishes, dioceses, schools, and charities, we had never before worked with a college chaplaincy. We told Chaplain Brewster we would be happy to assist with our development methodologies and experiences in the Episcopal Church. Underwritten as a Church Foundation grant, we led a development conference in New Orleans in the spring of 1997. More than twenty college chaplaincies were represented.

We covered the basics of fund raising including annual giving, planned giving, endowment building, and capital campaigns. While sharing information on fund raising with a dedicated group of chaplains and board members, we also discovered some interesting truths about college chaplaincies in our denomination.

Often, college chaplaincies are near the bottom of diocesan priorities. Of course, numerous dioceses energetically support their college chaplains and are assertive in reserving resources to maintain this ministry in as many colleges as possible. On the other hand, in many dioceses, chaplaincies have lost their financial support, have ceased to exist, or are marginal ministries.

We also learned that college chaplaincies come in all shapes, sizes, and models. Our mental image of the classic college chaplain with his or her own Canterbury House, ministering to an undergraduate population, proved to be outdated. In our work with several dozen college chaplaincies, we discovered that many co-exist with other congregations, and/or the chaplains serve as an assistant priest in a local parish. Just as often, a college chaplain shares offices and a chapel in an ecumenical center, rather than in a Canterbury House.

Last, we discovered many of our denomination chaplaincies were not raising annual giving funds for their particular ministries and very few had any endowment. To establish such programs, chaplains and boards must understand the basics of fund raising:

1. Annual Parish Stewardship
2. Capital Campaign
3. Planned Giving
4. Annual Giving for Agencies and Schools

Annual Parish Stewardship. The type of giving with which those of us in the church are most familiar is annual parish stewardship. These gifts are put in the collection plate on Sunday morning, and support the budget and ministry of our parishes. Obviously, annual parish stewardship is a challenge for a chaplaincy. Often the only congregation that a chaplain has is a student population, along with, in some cases, a few faculty or staff of the institution. Relatively few funds are donated by these groups to college chaplaincies.

Capital Campaign. The second form of giving is the capital campaign, which is used when a chaplaincy or any other part of the Episcopal Church needs to purchase property, build a new building, or remodel or renovate an existing structure. In some cases, focused capital drives also include the building of an endowment. Endowment is a permanent savings account, the income of which is used, but not the principal.

Planned Giving. Planned giving is the encouraging of gifts through bequests in wills or life income gifts such as pooled income funds or charitable remainder trusts, life insurance, real estate, or any gift from appreciated property. Chaplaincies are encouraged to work closely with their diocesan planned giving officer or a representative of the Episcopal Church Foundation to market and establish such gifts.

Annual Giving. This is not to be confused with annual parish stewardship. Annual giving encourages supporters of a particular agency, school, or charity to help support the budgetary needs of that ministry. For example, all of us receive requests through the mail to give to the Salvation Army at Christmas time or from our alma maters asking for donations. In our work with college chaplaincies across the country, we have observed that almost without exception, all could initiate an annual giving program for their ministry or could upgrade an existing program.

Let us examine how one strengthens a college chaplaincy through annual giving.

Establish an Annual Giving Program

Identify Your Need
No one can raise funds—annual giving or capital efforts—without first articulating why gifts are needed. Several chaplaincies with which we have worked faced declining diocesan support. For many chaplaincies, the need is paramount to increase annual support that underwrites the general budget or to enhance and expand programming. Begin by identifying your need, document it, and prepare to broadcast the news of your ministry. In some cases, there are significant construction needs or a desire to build endowment. First the board must articulate the need and establish consensus.

Establish a Mini-Development Office
After the need, or vision, has been articulated, it must be communicated. Establish a small development office. Create a modest budget that will include employing someone to enter and maintain the names and addresses of your growing constituency in a database for your mailing list. Hire someone, perhaps part time, with computer skills to get started. Provide a clerical space that includes access to a photocopier and fax machine. Create a budget for postage, meal meetings, and above all, publications.

Prices for development offices can vary from an investment of $5,000 to $10,000 for the first year plus modest secretarial assistance. This investment can cost considerably more if you have an aggressive program and a growing constituency.

Establish a Database of Potential Donors
It is vitally important to maintain a database with accurate giving records and addresses of the people whose lives have been affected by the ministry. Input the names, addresses, e-mail addresses, and phone contacts of the constituents that support your ministry. These could be:

- current-day students
- alumni
- faculty
- staff of the university
- parents of current students
- parents of previously enrolled students
- parishioners of a supporting parish(es)
- the parishes of the dioceses
- all diocesan clergy

- individual parishioners who have expressed a strong interest in your activities

- all diocesan officers

- your growing list of friends

Use parish and diocesan directories to find names and addresses. Also enter the names and addresses of those who attended the last diocesan convention or who serve on diocesan committees or councils. As a chaplain, don't hesitate to put the names and addresses of your friends and new acquaintances in the database. You can always remove the names later. Input the name of every Episcopal alumnus you can. Collect names of alumni at each reunion and diocesan convention.

Maintaining this database is crucial. This is the main task for the secretary who should constantly update records, change addresses, add new names, and delete those who don't respond to your newsletter or request for donation. We know of one chaplain who discovered in the church basement names of alumni from classes a half-century earlier. He raced to the college alumni office to research addresses of living alumni, and he immediately wrote to them. A number responded with gifts and nostalgic notes.

Build a Strong Chaplaincy Board

Many chaplaincy boards are weak or non-existent. In our travels across the country, we have observed some strong boards and some not-so-strong boards. Some boards meet regularly and some rarely meet at all. Make yours as strong as possible.

The bishop appoints some boards; some elect themselves. Some board members are selected because they have had a working or social relationship with the chaplain in some other venue. Appoint people who have a deep interest in what you are trying to accomplish. Board members should be able to give time and energy, and eventually financial resources to strengthen the ministry.

Boards need to be composed of three types of people: those who will work, those who have wisdom, and those who have wealth. We call these attributes "the three Ws." A good board needs some of each. There is also an axiom about board membership: "Give, Get, or Get off." Boards are critical to the financial stability of the organization.

It is important to have a mix of clergy and laity in order to balance your board. Clergy who represent other parishes are crucial because they have the ability to explain to their communities what the chaplaincy is trying to accomplish. Invite alumni to serve, and ask people with networking ability to join your board. No matter how you assemble your board, keep in mind how important it is for its members to communicate their witness of the ministry as well as financially underwrite the chaplaincy.

Increase Communication

We have noticed that almost all chaplains spend some time getting out a newsletter to the student body and the faculty that they are serving. A chaplain must also publish and mail a newsletter to the constituency that is off campus. If potential supporters do not know of the ministry, they cannot be moved to make gifts.

Print and mail regularly a newsletter to your growing constituency, including those whose names and addresses constantly being added to the database. The newsletter must include a response donation envelope, which need not be expensive or extravagant. Pre-addressed giving envelopes should go in every newsletter for easy return to the chaplaincy. Offer potential donors a box to check that encourages them to give $35, $50, $75, $100, or more. Identify how funds will be used.

Set up a website if you can afford it. Websites are invaluable tools, providing easy access to important information. Instant communication save time and effort, so create an e-mail address book; however, do not substitute e-mails for newsletters with response envelopes. It is still challenging to give over the Internet, and most donors continue to give via the postal service.

You must increase the visibility of your chaplaincy. Don't take for granted that the parishioners in your diocese know that your chaplaincy exists. You may be the recipient of funds from the diocese, from a parish or parishes, or from the endowment fund of the diocese. But it is important that you continue to be visible and share the good news of the work of your chaplaincy with every member of your diocese. Do not hide your light under a bushel. A bishop is under much stress to find the resources to support many worthy causes within a diocese. Do not take for granted that he or she knows the status of your work, the number of people that you assist with pastoral care, or how many lives have been touched by the work that you are doing. Share the good news; bishops hear enough bad news! It is a joy when someone comes into the office or drops a note and lets them know how well things are going.

Don't overlook the diocesan council or finance committee, the members who prepare the annual budget for the diocese. Keep them informed about how things are going and how your work is changing the lives of young people.

If a parish is helping to sponsor your program directly, either because you share facilities or it is a regular contributor, make sure you share with the vestry and parishioners the many ongoing activities of the ministry, even ones as simple as you or a college student speaking from the pulpit or in an adult forum. Put everyone in the parish on your mailing list. Let them know what's going on and how well their gifts are furthering the ministry of the church.

When you go to a diocesan convention, ask for time on the agenda to address the convention. Set up a booth in the exhibit area and staff it with students. Hang posters and photographs. Tell over and over the story of what the college chaplaincy is doing on the campus that you represent.

Consider creating a speaker's bureau, consisting of the chaplain, perhaps some of your more talented students, and members of your board. They need to speak often to the parishes in your diocese (especially those who have you in their budget directly), women's groups, men's clubs, and Sunday morning adult forums.

In any form or fashion you can think of, be part of diocesan communication. If your diocese has a website, ask to be included or linked. It is a relatively inexpensive way to get the word out. If the parish to which you are assigned has a website, attach a chaplaincy page. Send regular stories to the diocesan newspaper and to your local paper. Communicate the story in as many ways as you can. If people don't know about the chaplaincy, they will not be moved to send money when you ask. Tell your story now so the gifts will come later.

Execute the Annual Giving Program

With your database established and your communication program in high gear, you should:

- Mail to your donor base or constituency base several times a year. Here is a sample calendar:

Date	Activity
September	Mail newsletter with response envelope.
Late November	Mail letter from board president, bishop, or yourself with a response envelope asking people directly for funds.
May	Mail end-of-school-year newsletter, again with response envelope.

- Consider sponsoring a special fund-raising event: Hold a tailgate party before a home football game. Have an open house during homecoming. When the Universities of Kansas and Kansas State play their big annual football game, the two respective Canterbury clubs face each other on their own gridiron in a game of touch football. They use the occasion to sell tickets and raise money. The chaplaincy at Princeton hosts an open house at each May reunion.

- Asking is the best way of raising money, and not just sending a letter, but calling people and asking one-on-one. We know the most effective fund-raising method in the United States of America is simply seeing people face to face and asking, "Can you join me in supporting this ministry? Would you please include our ministry in your annual giving plans for the coming year?" Not hard to do. Just take time to enter into some type of relationship and information sharing with the people that you are calling on. It will require commitment to make visits, share information, and ask for a response. In your budget, set aside funds to use for lunch meetings for these purposes.

■ Ask for gift levels in your newsletter. Set up a $100-a-year club, or ask certain people to join at a $1,000-a-year giving level. It can be done. Episcopalians are generous, but if you don't ask, you don't receive, whereas you have everything to gain by asking. Our denominational giving is among the highest in the United States. Of course many Episcopalians give outside of their parishes and donate generously to museums, hospitals, and alma maters. Why shouldn't they give to your ministry as well? If you've properly shared information and the potential donors are aware of your need, then you are ready to ask them to respond.

■ Call on parishes. Have you exhausted all the possibilities of visiting the parishes that have historically supported you? What about the parishes that are located within easy driving distance of your campus or university? Don't assume that folks know about you or that they know your need for funds. When you speak to adult forums or make visits to vestries, tell your story and request that your ministry be included in the annual giving programs.

■ Keep the financial entities that support your ministry constantly informed of what's happening with your campaign.

Say Thank You

With your annual giving program moving forward, it is important to send out regular thank-you notes and acknowledgments. As gifts are received, it is critical that they are recorded in your database and that personal responses are sent as quickly as possible. Try to avoid computer-generated thank-you notes. One chaplain we know sends a personal, handwritten note for each gift. At the very least, include a postscript, thanking donors for what they have done and will make possible, and personally sign all letters. Make sure that the development secretary records the giving history of all donors and sends the appropriate year-end letter of contributions to all those who have made a gift of $250 or more in that calendar year, as required by the Internal Revenue Service.

Publish the names of all donors in one of your newsletters. If you have used giving levels in your campaign, you could include a section for those who donated $100 and above, a section for $500 and above, and one higher. Whereas one would not publish a list of donors for one's parish, this is permissible in a

college chaplaincy. If it troubles you to list the names, you certainly don't have
to, but it is an appropriate practice. Some donors may request anonymity
at the outset, in which case, of course, they should be left off this list.

How to Launch a Capital or Endowment Campaign for Your Chaplaincy

Until now, we have been discussing the importance of annual giving, the regular contributions that flow into your chaplaincy, usually as a result of direct
mail, although sometimes through special events and often from visiting
constituents. But now your chaplaincy has a special need: Canterbury House
is in need of repairs, or maybe it's time to look for a new property. Perhaps
your ministry has come to the point that it needs its own facility, and it is
time to leave the supporting parish. The process of raising such extraordinary funds is called a capital campaign.

Some chaplaincies may consider formal endowment drives. Numerous
chaplaincies across the country are attempting to build or increase endowment,
the income from which can underwrite the ministry for decades to come.

As previously mentioned, the three chief components of capital or endowment drives are:

1. Discernment
2. Feasibility Study
3. Gifting Phase

A capital drive is a bit like an order of worship: there is a process to it. It
has a beginning (an invocation) and an end (a benediction), and in the middle are a number of activities that are critical to the process.

Institute a Discernment Process

As with other types of campaigns, the first step is the discernment process. If
capital needs are anticipated, an Exploration Committee should be appointed
from the board. You might also go outside the board and involve others in the
process to help discern the chaplaincy needs for capital restoration, improvement, building, or establishing or enhancing an endowment. Articulate the
proposed plans on paper. It's amazing how many church groups talk continuously about possibilities but fail to lay out a concrete plan in writing. If you
put it on paper, then you can do the next step, which is sharing the proposed
plans with as large a constituency as possible. Always ask for feedback.

Communicate often and aggressively with your constituency. Through
your newsletter, tell folks that you are wrestling with a possible capital campaign. Tell your bishop. Tell your convention. Tell your supporting parishes.
Tell all your prospective donors and donors on record what you are doing.

Publish your findings in the diocesan newspaper. Never assume that the public is aware of campaign activities.

It is also important to pray about the process, to discern whether your chaplaincy is being called to do God's work in this effort. Such a campaign is not a thing of vanity or an activity to improve one's career track; rather, it is a calling from God to further God's ministry.

Conduct a Feasibility Study

After you have engaged your constituency in a dialogue, invited their responses, and informed them of what's happening, it is time to solicit a formal response. An official survey is needed to discover (1) whether the constituency favors the proposed project; and (2) to what extent the members would be financially supportive.

For chaplaincies, feasibility studies involve hiring outside consultants who will interview a number of people one-on-one. The consultant will usually also insist that you send the same questionnaire and proposed plans to everyone on your mailing list. With responses in hand, experienced consultants can draw conclusions about the ability of your chaplaincy to harvest appropriate funds for a capital or endowment drive.

The study itself usually takes two to three months to accomplish, even if you've already spent one, two, or even three years on the discernment process. The study is a wise investment, as it will answer important questions: Are you ready for a campaign? Are people ready to give? Are leadership gifts available to help make your vision a reality? If the study is positive, you are ready to move to the capital solicitation phase.

Conduct a Capital Solicitation

Conducting a capital solicitation for college chaplaincies can be challenging. It's not just a parish campaign, a diocesan campaign, or a campaign for the alumni of the university, but instead a combination of all three. Putting it all together is a major undertaking that will require a great deal of work from the college chaplain and the lay volunteers who give themselves to the task. The process normally takes five to seven months, possibly eight to ten, from start to finish.

Preparation and planning are required before you act. You must recruit leadership and publish materials describing what is proposed. You must ask major donor prospects to give first. Eventually the process moves to a general gift solicitation, offering alumni, parents of students, students, faculty, staff, and parishes the opportunity to participate in the drive.

Generally, you will need outside help to assist in putting together and managing such an activity. Seek a fund-raising consultant who has been through the process before, can set deadlines, and will ensure that the solicitation is accomplished in a timely fashion. Select a consultant who approaches his or her work as ministry and not merely fund raising.

A Word about Endowment

Chaplaincies across the country have their own chaplaincy endowment committees or foundations. Others rely on a local parish, and still others on the diocese. These committees, parishes, and dioceses see that the funds are properly supervised, managed, and appropriated. Some critical questions that you should address in advance are:

- Who will be responsible for selecting the financial institution that will invest the money for the chaplaincy?

- What is a prudent yet appropriate investment of the funds? How much can we expect in income each year?

- Who will oversee the budget process in general? Can the endowment ever be invaded?

- Is the endowment only for the college chaplaincy or also for other ministries?

Record your answers to these questions, and make sure that you have a highly credible group of lay and clergy who are supervising what you are doing.

What Can Be Accomplished?

Feeling overwhelmed? By this time you are coming to understand that a college chaplain in the twenty-first century is a demanding position. In addition to exercising your ministry, you must also invest part of your time in maintaining and advancing the ministry.

Still, you should now be able to establish a development office, execute an annual giving program, and/or initiate a capital drive. With your board, prepare a plan and execute as much as you can when you can. Walk before you run, but take the first steps.

Help Is Available

As a result of our ongoing work over the years with college chaplaincies and the Episcopal Church Foundation, we recommended the establishment of a national college chaplaincy development office to assist chaplains. Underwritten by the Episcopal Church Foundation, CampuSource, Inc. has been established as a not-for-profit development office. An e-mail or phone call will result in a helping hand, at a very reasonable fee, to assist the advancement of any college ministry. We tip our hat to the Episcopal Church Foundation for backing this important endeavor. Contact CampuSource at Info@CampuSource.com. The staff can be of tremendous help.

ELEVEN

Establishing a Church Planned Giving Program

EDITOR'S NOTE: Glenn Holliman, who left the world of independent education in 1982 to become one of the first diocesan planned giving officers in the Episcopal Church, writes this chapter. His earlier and comprehensive treatment on planned giving, entitled "The Complete Planned Giving Kit," which includes The Planned Giving Guide for Churches, *a video, numerous track rack brochures, and bulletin inserts, is available through Morehouse Publishing.*

As we illustrated earlier with our three-legged stool, the third leg of a mature church resource development program (after annual stewardship and capital campaigns) is planned giving. Planned giving is an encompassing term that includes:

- bequests in wills
- life income gifts such as:
  - pooled income funds
  - charitable gift annuities
  - charitable remainder trusts
- life insurance
- life estates and gifts of real estate
- charitable lead trusts
- bargain sales

Any gift that requires assistance from an advisor could be called a planned gift. Often these gifts are "deferred" in that they do not pass immediately to a church or charity, as would an outright gift. Most gifts pass to the church at the death of the donor or other beneficiary, hence they are deferred.

Although a bequest in a will is the most common method to remember the church in estate planning, many are attracted to the benefits of life income gifts. At this writing, the charitable gift annuity has particular appeal, paying relative high rates of guaranteed returns to donors.

Indeed, as startling as it sounds, one can give away one's resources to the church, receive an income for life with a tax deduction, and receive some income tax-free. At the death of the final beneficiary, an annuity remainder goes to that part of the church the donor so designates. During times of low interest rates, annuity returns can be very attractive. People can literally give away their money and increase their incomes. Variations of the charitable gift annuity include charitable remainder trusts and pooled income funds.

Enabling these life income gifts in the Episcopal Church is the task of the Episcopal Church Foundation at the Church Center in New York, with its extensive program of education and facilitation. *Funding Future Ministry*, co-written by Fred Osborne, the Reverend Charles Gearing, and Pam Wesley, is a comprehensive guide and exploration of how churches can facilitate and develop planned giving programs. It also lists the services offered by the Foundation. Visit their website at www.EpiscopalFoundation.Org. Foundation representatives can assist your parish and diocese with information and facilitation.

With this brief introduction, let me challenge and encourage you, before going further into this subject, to be scripturally and theologically grounded. As we know, the Jesus of the Gospels challenges us to be in harmony with our Creator and fellow humans. Another great theme of the New Testament is our proper relationship to material wealth. As we have noted, many of the parables of Jesus, such as The Rich Fool in Luke 12:16–21, are directed at issues of wealth and worldly goods. The Rich Fool built a business and estate only to discover, as everyone does, that death will claim us all.

The American entrepreneurial spirit is uncomfortable with the message of The Rich Fool. Our capitalist society encourages us to create additional wealth and accumulate possessions. The Gospels exist to pull us back into balance, reminding us that we are creatures, not the Creator, and all that we have is held in trust to pass along to future generations. The writer of 1 Chronicles 29:14a, states it well: "For all things come from thee, [O God,] and of thy own have we given thee." Approach your planned giving program as a ministry, a time to call people to examine their theology of stewardship, to seek the balance between things of this world and the everlasting richness of being in harmony with God's love.

I have studied the work and writings of the Reverend Charles Gearing of Atlanta, Georgia, a pioneer in the Episcopal denomination in planned giving. Let us adapt our concept of a three-legged stool for planned giving (with apologies to Charles for some changes in concepts).

Planned Giving

Vision   Marketing

Policies

First a Vision

As Proverbs records, without a vision, the people perish. Before embarking on a planned giving program, draft a proposal of how endowment or received planned gifts could or would be used. The results of their giving a substantial sum to the church must be made obvious to congregation members, who are also likely being asked to give to colleges, hospitals, museums, and the like. Articulate clearly the ministries that could be enhanced and initiated.

Unfortunately, too often a bequest is received in a church that has no vision or policy in place. I remember a meeting one morning with a priest in the Midwest on behalf of his diocese. The priest was affable and animated, stating he had just received notification from an attorney that a deceased member had left the church over one million dollars, many times the annual budget.

"Wonderful!" I said, thinking perhaps there might be a tithe to the diocesan campaign I represented. "What will you do with it?"

"I have no idea." he replied, "This has never happened before!"

What a delightful opportunity that was for building an endowment to produce income for:

- outreach

- Christian education and youth

- maintenance on an aging physical plant

- music or other special ministries specific to your mission

Before you are surprised by a similar letter from an attorney, involve the leadership and congregation of your church in exploring needs and opportunities. Ask as many people as possible to help shape the vision, and give people a sense of ownership. They are much more likely to remember the church in their estate if they had the opportunity to help define the vision.

Policies

The second leg of the strong planned giving program is the setting of policies-written statements, approved by the vestry, indicating how funds in endowment are to be used, managed, and distributed. Several years ago, during a planned giving program in the Diocese of Central New York, I posed these questions to church leaders. Does your church have the answers, in writing, to these questions?

- Who will determine how endowment funds are to be used?

- Who will manage them and distribute them?

- How much income can be distributed and to which ministries?

- Can principle be involved or borrowed?

- Can policies be altered?

You may be surprised that your leadership has not addressed many of these issues, but don't worry, you don't have to invest in expensive legal help. The Episcopal Church Foundation has published draft policies for your church's adaptation. Give them a call.

Control of money can be a source of conflict in a church, as evidenced in the Bible. Some time ago, I visited a distraught rector in a southern parish. For four decades, one person dominated the supervision and distribution of sizeable income from the church's endowment. His status in the community and church was such that no rector for decades had been able to question, much less change the income stream for the account. An unhealthy and frustrating situation, you can imagine. Make sure you have a rotating leadership and vestry democracy when dealing with large sums of money. Put your policies on paper and review them from time to time.

Unfortunately, too many churches have suffered when fiduciary responsibility has been violated and endowment considerably reduced or in some cases stolen, due to poor oversight by committees and vestries. Conduct annual audits.

Marketing

Don't be put off by this secular word. We have to tell the story. We have to share the vision and ask for donations. Sharing the vision is exciting, but asking people to remember the church in their wills usually slows most of us down.

Writing a will is an important event in life. It reminds us all that we are mortal. We are also forced to sum up what we have and how our wealth is to be distributed. This decision can be a painful one. Are some heirs more disadvantaged or more deserving than others? Most of us are forced to acknowledge that life is not always kind and that families have divisions and unresolved hurts. Therefore, advocates of planned giving should approach their work as ministry, not fund raising. Encouraging people to write (with professional help) their own wills is an act of ministry. Surviving family members experience heartache at the death of a loved one; why allow them to experience headaches from legal and financial confusion as well? Preparing a will while in good health is an act of love.

Share the church vision, encourage creating an up-to-date will, and offer like-income gift examples. From time to time, people will include the church in their estate and financial plans, and over the years the endowment will grow. Hold seminars, send mailings, and speak often on the subject.

Want to be more ambitious? Form a Legacy Society. Invite founding members to express in writing that they have remembered the church in their will or through life insurance, a gift annuity, or other instrument

What Can Be Accomplished?

We all scramble to find resources for outreach, or youth programs, or building repairs. Creating an endowment through planned giving can be an effective and dynamic method to further ministry. You can assist families in final planning and help establish resources for greater ministry. Make planned giving a viable and important part of your "three-legged stool" of church development.

TWELVE

What to Expect from Your Church Architect

by Kenneth M. Graves, AIA

WE HAVE ASKED OUR Episcopal colleague, Kenneth M. Graves, an architect in San Antonio, Texas, to write this chapter. Ken has assisted churches, schools, businesses, and individuals in planning wisely for new construction. In addition to being a fine architect, he is a dedicated Christian and former Senior Warden at Saint Luke's Episcopal Church in San Antonio, Texas. Although this chapter revolves around church construction, the steps outlined apply to any church school or church agency.

Consider the following: A good architect and proper planning can go a long way toward ensuring that any construction or restoration will best serve the ministries of your church, school, or agency.

Before you turn a spade full of dirt or hammer a nail, ask yourself if your church has the following:

1. A building committee: a group representing a cross section of all interested parties, the official church leadership, the staff, committee chair persons, and all age groups. (Don't forget to include those with construction and/or engineering experience.) The committee should communicate with the rest of the congregation throughout the entire planning process. Gaps in communication can cause problems further into the program.
2. A master plan: a comprehensive written plan created by your architect that reflects your vision.
3. A realistic budget: a financial outline that articulates what is achievable through fund raising and borrowing to complete your vision. It is important to have a vision, but the vision must coincide with financial reality. How much is in your building fund? How much can or do you wish to raise from a capital campaign and/or borrowing?

The Need for an Architect

An architect can be compared to the conductor of a symphony orchestra. It is the conductor who coordinates the musicians and brings their individual talents together to produce harmonious music. Like a conductor, an architect is trained to be the overall director for myriad disciplines that go into planning and constructing a building. It is his/her expertise that will pull all individuals into the cohesive team that will work toward your project's completion.

The architect also works with many other professionals as on a team. These professionals will produce required documents and plans. (Architects are licensed by the state, and place their names and State Registration Seals on all documents that are produced, so they are ultimately responsible for the plans.) Depending on the size and complexity of your project, other professionals involved may include a civil engineer, structural engineer, mechanical engineer, electrical engineer, plumbing engineer, interior designer, and/or landscape architect.

How to Find an Architect

Interview architects who are recommended to you and who have experience in church design. If the architect is already familiar with liturgical language, you will spend less time explaining the meaning of terms and theological symbolism. Also, the architect should know from experience what spaces are required and how large they need to be. Ask other churches for recommendations or talk to friends who have worked with architects.

Invite each recommended architect to submit a statement of interest to your committee. This is normal procedure and provides you with detailed résumés outlining work experience. From these submittals, you can develop a list of architects to invite for an interview.

Selecting an Architect

The interview will tell you how well your personalities are going to work together. Pick an architect that your committee is comfortable with, since you will be working closely with this person for a number of months and relying on his or her judgment. Request references and follow through.

Hire an architect only after your leadership has agreed on the following:

- The personalities will work well together.

- You have confidence in the architect's advice and will accept it based on his or her experience.

- You have verified through previous clients that the architect comes to you well recommended.

- You understand what the architect will be doing and how much it will cost to develop your plans.

Fees. During the interview process, it is important to discuss the hourly fee or compensation arrangements. Architects often charge an hourly fee plus expenses. The hourly rate may differ based on experience, size of the firm, and/or complexity of the project. In some locations, expect to pay a percentage of the cost of the project (the signed contract amount). This could be as much as 18 percent for a remodeling project or as little as 6 percent for new construction.

Turn Words into Space

Your Capital Needs Committee should sufficiently prepare basic information for your architect to get started. First, arrange for an up-to-date survey of your property that includes any improvements, the property lines, contour lines, trees, and any easements or setbacks on the land. The legal description is required to obtain a building permit. Not having this information readily available will delay the process.

Needs Assessment

The architect usually conducts a needs assessment by interviewing each member of the staff and chairs of committees. He or she will also meet with the building committee to study the proposed vision. This assessment process assists the architect in better understanding how the building spaces are currently used. The architect will then develop a program for the committee to follow in setting priorities. It will also serve as a checklist throughout the planning process as problems are identified and solutions proposed.

The Design

The architect will work from the written program to produce a schematic design that will later serve as your master plan. He or she is trained to view space in the most efficient way possible. The Right Reverend Jeffery Rowthorn, former Episcopal Bishop of the American Convocation in Europe, has remarked: "It has been said that an architect looks at a building and sees what is not there, while the layman looks at the building and sees only what is there."

The architect also has a wealth of experience and knowledge about construction principals and design that will play a large role in the development of your plans. Remember that the architect works every day with building codes, laws, and legal requirements and therefore understands how all of these factors may impact your building design.

Expect to have a series of meetings with the architect in which ideas will be presented for your reaction and input. It is this interaction with the architect that will lead to a consensus for the design of the building. As state in previous chapters, the agreed-upon design should be shared with all interested people in your congregation. Start with your church leadership, and then hold a general meeting with the congregation. Allow the architect to make his/her own presentation. Input from these meetings will enhance the design, and the plans will be more accepted once everyone is involved in the process.

The accepted preliminary plan is your master plan and usually includes everything you would like to have built. It should also include the estimated costs of the proposed project. However, can your church afford this vision? This question brings you to the next step—the feasibility study.

Feasibility Study

As noted earlier, a thorough study will provide a great deal of needed information, especially in answering the question, "How much can we raise?" It will allow your committee to set a realistic budget for your program and will help prioritize the elements in your plan according to the responses from your congregation.

After a study, either you will be able to move forward, confident that your vision can become a reality, or you will adjust your plans to correspond with the giving potential of your congregation and constituencies. In many cases, projects are completed with a combination of financial borrowing and capital drives. Ascertain how much debt your congregation can finance and whether loans are available at reasonable rates.

Conduct a Capital Campaign

With the feasibility study results and a master plan in place, you can now conduct your capital campaign. With the campaign accomplished and any needed financing in place, the building process can now proceed.

Hire a Construction Architect

You are not required to use the architect who created the master plan for construction. Sometimes a different firm may adopt the master plan concepts and follow the project through to completion. You may have hired the first architect because he or she was a visionary designer, while another architect was recommended as a production-oriented professional. You may even choose to have the first architect joint-venture the project with a second architect, joining the visionary artist with a nuts-and-bolts production firm.

The architect will sign an "AIA Contract between Owner and Architect." This document fully explains what the responsibilities are for each party. It details the phases of the architect's work and is the best resource your committee can review prior to hiring the architect. You can obtain a copy by contacting your local AIA (American Institute of Architects) office. There is a nominal charge for the document. The following are brief summaries of the work phases:

1. *Preliminary Design:* The architect will once again review the program requirements and include in the design drawings any legal requirements such as code compliance, handicap accessibility, special considerations for neighbors, etc.

   Remember that constant communication is the key to successfully completing a project. This includes communicating with any adjacent property owners. Sharing development information is not required by law, but it can prevent any misunderstandings that could lead to legal problems and/or objections from neighbors when you apply for a building permit.

2. *Design Development:* Finishing details such as closets, storage, walls, lighting, and any other special requirements are discussed and put into the plans. This is also when additional engineers become involved in the project for the first time. Your preliminary cost estimate can be reviewed during this phase of the work since the plans will be more complete. The various disciplines can also verify costs for their particular area. The newly detailed cost estimate will allow your committee to review the project and reset priorities accordingly. These final revised plans should be presented to the leadership and the congregation.

3. *Construction Documents:* Written specifications must be drawn to further define how space is to be divided and used according to the vision of the architect. This phase will result in technical drawings that are less easily read by non-professionals.

   The architect coordinates the work done by all the engineers to create a set of bid documents. The bidding process is similar to hiring an architect. Invite only those contractors whom you would potentially hire. Your architect should be able to recommend appropriate contractor candidates. Many factors should be considered; therefore, rely on your architect's advice.

4. *Construction Administration:* This is considered by architects to be the key to the successful completion of a project. The architect is again your best guide during this critical part of the project, as he or she best understands the overall concept of your building. It is the architect who can tell you whether a proposed material is equal to the one specified in the plans. He or she can also advise you on the percentage of work actually completed so you do not over-pay for construction.

Leaving these details to the architect frees your committee to resolve other problems and considerations. For example, during the construction period, you may be able to move about within your building or you may need to vacate your building altogether. Either way, extra costs should be budgeted.

Planning and building are always a challenge. Working with an architect skilled in church building will make your job as church leaders easier and will ensure that you are being good stewards of the funds entrusted to your committee.

Review of the Steps for a Successful Building Project

1. Write a mission statement defining who you are and what you are about as a church.
2. Write a long-range plan articulating the ministries your church wishes to conduct and how they would be accomplished through new construction, renovation, or remodeling.
3. Establish a building committee that includes representatives from all groups within the congregation.
4. Employ an architect to create a master plan that turns your words into space and then share these plans with the congregation.
5. Undertake a feasibility study to determine your ability to raise funds.
6. Conduct a capital campaign that, along with possible financing, establishes your achievable budget.
7. Instruct the architect to finalize the plans.
8. Consider other professionals you may need to hire, such as an interior designer or landscape architect, etc.
9. Place a bid with a contractor and build the building.
10. Bracket all of the above with prayer for church and congregation as you seek to know and do the will of God.

EPILOGUE

WE HAVE COVERED much material to this point. The task before you may seem daunting and overwhelming. Remember that each day, church leaders, school heads, and executive directors of church agencies make critical decisions to move forward:

- To increase and expand ministries.

- To restore and renew older facilities.

- To construct new facilities.

- To build endowment for maintenance and programming.

- To find extraordinary funds for new ministries and service.

Remember the example of Moses in the wilderness when he sought the materials to construct his portable temple. Seek to know first what God would have you to do. Then using those God-given talents of organization, communication, and the ability to lead, go forth and accomplish increased ministry and service in your time and place.

If we are about the work of God, and if people have heard the word of God, then faithful people will respond "with generous hearts."